Back Where I Came From

BACK WHERE I

Back Where I Came F...

CAME FROM

ON CULTURE, IDENTITY, AND HOME

edited by TASLIM JAFFER and OMAR MOUALLEM

ESSAIS NO. 17

BOOK*HUG PRESS
TORONTO 2024

Library and Archives Canada Cataloguing in Publication

Title: Back where I came from : on culture, identity, and home /
    edited by Taslim Jaffer and Omar Mouallem.
Names: Jaffer, Taslim, 1978– editor. | Mouallem, Omar, 1985– editor.
Description: Series statement: Essais series
Identifiers: Canadiana (print) 20240335104 | Canadiana (ebook) 20240335260
ISBN 9781771669177 (softcover) | ISBN 9781771669221 (EPUB)
Subjects: LCSH: Authors, Canadian—Travel. | LCSH: Authors, American—Travel.
    LCSH: Travel—Socialaspects. | LCSH: Travel—Political aspects. | LCSH: Travel—
    Humor. LCSH: Cultural awareness. |LCGFT: Essays.
Classification: LCC PS8367.T72 B33 2024 | DDC C814/.6—dc23

The production of this book was made possible through the generous assistance of the Canada Council for the Arts and the Ontario Arts Council. Book*hug Press also acknowledges the support of the Government of Canada through the Canada Book Fund and the Government of Ontario through the Ontario Book Publishing Tax Credit and the Ontario Book Fund.

Book*hug Press acknowledges that the land on which we operate is the traditional territory of many nations, including the Mississaugas of the Credit, the Anishnabeg, the Chippewa, the Haudenosaunee, and the Wendat peoples. We recognize the enduring presence of many diverse First Nations, Inuit, and Métis peoples, and are grateful for the opportunity to meet, work, and learn on this territory.

for our parents,
and for all the people and places we came from

Contents

TASLIM JAFFER AND OMAR MOUALLEM

Introduction

This book was born from the mutual curiosity of two children of immigrants about the experiences of diasporic writers who've travelled back to their, or their parents', or in some cases grandparents', countries of origin. As writers ourselves who had journeyed back to our motherlands, we wanted to find the common threads between storytellers with an array of backgrounds, and where, and why, those common threads ended. Did they, like us, bump up against uncomfortable questions about themselves when they visited their ancestral lands? Did they return with a renewed sense of belonging, home, and identity? And could we artistically represent these narratives, give them their rightful space in English literature, and shed some light on the joys and struggles of being from both "here" and "there"?

We put out a submission call to the writing community and received over one hundred thoughtful submissions detailing travels across the globe and the full gamut of emotions experienced in diasporas. The abstract space between cultures, where many hyphenated Canadians and Americans live, opened up as writers delved into the contrast between home and homeland, to unpack family matters, politics, heartbreaks, health issues, and themselves. Writers did not shy away from vulnerability

1

in sharing with us their dreams—both dashed and fulfilled—and often sent their essays with a note of thanks for the opportunity to put on the page some meaningful, difficult, or gratifying experiences. "Writing this was a joy," one author said, "and even if it's not selected, I'm more than grateful to have spent this time putting into words something even my wife did not fully know." The essay "Chicken Soup and Tortillas" by Omar Reyes is an endearing tale of classism and self-discovery in El Salvador, one of the twenty-four countries you will travel to as you read this book.

We envisioned an anthology that would showcase rich and vivid storytelling from around the globe. We welcomed writers who came at our themes of culture, identity, and home from slightly different angles; in "Flight Paths" Omar El Akkad recounts his life of multiple migrations in the wake of his father's death, while in "Dépaysement" Christina Hoag shows what it's like growing up a third-culture kid with relative privilege but no ties to any one country.

It was clear that stories of travel would include ideas about land and the institutions that govern them. In "The Land Remembers All of Its Children," Hannah Zalaa-Uul names Mongolia "a timeless mother" who welcomes her home no matter how long she has been away, no matter how much of a cultural outsider she feels she is. This idea is echoed in Alexandra C. Yeboah's poetic essay "The Motherland Knows My Name" about Ghana and the many ways she's told she is not African enough. Ayesha Habib, in "What Remains of Home," acknowledges the complicated history between a wave of Indian migrants driven from their homes and the native population of East Africa under Britain's imposed segregation. Which brings us to the countries that we, the editors and writers of this book, now live in, and our own history of settler-colonialism that we reconcile with in our own ways. In this spirit, we hear from Alison Tedford Seaweed, a member of the Kwakiutl First Nation of northern Vancouver Island, who experiences a homecoming that deepens her ties with her Indigenous identity, and Israeli-Canadian Lishai Peel, in "Mother, Land," who finds her way back to her mom and homeland after distancing herself from her government's "violent occupation of Palestinian territory," recognizing that "there was no escaping the person who made me and the country that shaped me."

Family relationships are another strong theme woven throughout this collection. Eufemia Fantetti makes a trek to Bonefro, Italy, after thirty-six years of estrangement from the land and her family there—"Imagine the guilt," she says before discovering a new understanding of past family trauma. Nhung N. Tran-Davies makes "The Journey Home" to Vietnam with her mother through a medical school opportunity and returns with greater knowledge of her mother's background that answers questions about her own difficult upbringing.

At a time when the discussion about rights to lay claim to a land is in the spotlight, when people are paying attention to the diversity of human experiences, we are proud to add context and nuance to the conversation. This is a book of dualities: of commonalities and eclecticism, of connection and disconnection, of belonging and alienation.

The title for this book is meant to be a little tongue-in-cheek, a response to the not-so-creative directive hurled at immigrants (or perceived immigrants) to go back where they came from. Here are twenty-six writers who did just that and returned with an array of profound and complicated and funny and magical stories to tell. We welcome readers to lands far, far away and to places deep within our ideas of who we are, where we belong, and what "home" means to us.

ALISON TEDFORD SEAWEED

Alive in Alert Bay

Coming Home to the Big House

I got my first glimpse of Alert Bay, British Columbia, from a hospital bed. Common sense and geography would tell you that what I'm telling you is impossible, given that the hospital bed was 350 kilometres across the Salish Sea, in Maple Ridge, but I can assure you it's true. Sometimes the most meaningful truths start out as a mystery, and I feel like the magic of my ancestors isn't bound by the same rules about time and space.

I didn't know I was looking at my ancestors' seaside community until my grandparents pointed it out, the village on Cormorant Island, where my family's roots run deep. They'd come to visit me at Ridge Meadows Hospital when Grandma asked me the strangest question as I lay there in my bed: "Did you bring that painting with you?" I explained to her that people don't bring art with them to the hospital—especially not teenagers. I was fifteen years old and could scarcely remember to bring my house keys with me when I left the house, let alone a painting. I wondered what she meant and why she would even think to ask that.

She gestured to the artwork on the wall and explained, "That's a painting of a totem pole your great-great-grandfather carved." It seemed wild that it would happen to be hanging there in a room five hundred

5

kilometres from where the totem pole stood, but there it was. Grandma took the painting down and walked out to the nurse's station. She explained the personal connection to the art and audaciously asked if she could take it.

I can only imagine how bewildered the staff were by her request. That was Grandma, always clear about what she wanted, and I'm quite sure the staff had no manual to refer to for this kind of situation. They agreed and Grandma took the painting with her, only to return it to me framed with a photo of her and Grandpa standing in front of the actual totem pole in Alert Bay.

I took it as a sign that my ancestors were with me and wanted me to be okay. It couldn't have been a coincidence that a watercolour print depicting my family's art would be hanging there while I was recovering from my eating disorder. I had been fighting it for years, malnourished and unsteady on my feet with dizzy spells. I was prone to fainting and my condition had progressed to the point where, in the hospital, my bare feet only connected with the cold floor to go to and from the bathroom. That was on doctor's orders, lest I try to use them to exercise.

Though I had seen photographs of my great-grandfather's totem poles, I had never been to Alert Bay to see this one in person. I didn't know anything about the village of 450 people, and I was too deep in my own troubles to wonder about it much. Once I was released from the hospital, I hung the art in the entryway of my home. I would think about it every time I looked at the painting, but it would be years before I'd find myself on those shores.

By that time I was a mother myself, headed to Alert Bay on a business trip as a finance and data quality officer with the federal prison system. I was supposed to drive a member of the parole board to the airport to fly with me to Port Hardy, but I'd recently been in a car accident. My colleague's husband drove us to the airport instead, and when

I explained that my family was from the area, and gave my birth name, he told me a story about when he'd been the band manager of my family's reserve near Port Hardy, where he'd had many conversations with my great-grandfather.

When my colleague and I landed at our destination, she drove me through the reserve to see where our people had lived—and still do. It felt surreal to drive over the roads where my great-grandparents once walked, to be where they had been, and I imagined them there, recalling what their faces looked like in the snapshots in my photo album. I had pictures of them holding me, smiling at me, loving me in their arms, but they passed away when I was so small that I could not remember the sounds of their voices. I wondered what it would have been like to visit them there and to have had memories in and of this place.

We headed up to the ferry that would take us to Alert Bay. I checked into a hotel on a pier and fell asleep to the sounds of the waves crashing below. A log was entangled below the dock, and it thumped against the posts all night, reminding me of the way my grandpa learned to dance to the beat of a drumstick connecting with a hollow log.

We were in town for a community justice forum, and I met some community members attending the event to share their perspectives, who, upon learning who my grandfather was, explained to me how we were related. I knew my grandparents, aunts, uncles, and cousins on the mainland who gathered together at the holidays, but, until that moment, knew almost nothing about my extended family on Vancouver Island. Through their stories, smiles, and hugs, I saw the lines of my family tree filling out with indelible ink.

I explored the little town as much as I could during our short stay, eating at local restaurants, walking around, and taking pictures. I snapped a photo of the residential school my grandfather attended, a building that, a few years later, would be demolished for safety reasons. And, of course, I saw the totem pole with my own eyes.

It was strange to see the painting come to life. I took it all in from behind the graveyard's fence, which stood in protection of the graves and totems, standing in awe at a distance. So close and still so far, I wondered what it might feel like to touch the wood he carved, to feel the grain under my fingertips. The fence was there for good reason and there would be more appropriate times to get closer to his work. I was there to witness and that was enough.

The next day, I went back home to the Fraser Valley, unsure when I would be back. It was far away, I had a young son at home, and as a single parent I didn't have much of a travel budget, so the idea of returning was tempting but felt impractical. But even though I didn't have a timeline for my return, I knew for sure that one day I would.

Many years later, after I'd left the government job and started my own business, and after the pandemic hit, I found a way back to Alert Bay, in a sense. Scrolling through Instagram, I noticed the cultural centre in Alert Bay was offering Kwak'wala lessons online. Health orders precluded lessons happening in person, so even locals were attending lessons remotely, and it was opened up to anyone who wanted to learn the language. Though my grandfather is a fluent speaker who taught our language at a local university, I rarely heard it spoken. I only knew how to say "cow" and "thank you" and life never provided an opportunity to use the two together. Embarrassed at how little of my language I could speak, I wanted to learn how to have a conversation with my grandpa in our language.

At the start of the first lesson, I introduced myself to all the unfamiliar faces on my screen, and when I shared my birth name, our instructor smiled. "I am your auntie!" she exclaimed. Gesturing to her sisters in the meeting who were also teaching the language with her, she said, "These are all your aunties!" To be claimed by new family in this way felt like discovering the beginning of a new and glorious chapter, full of cultural context, hope, and possibility, with all the weight that comes with having to write a new life story.

This was just after the 215 gravesites had been confirmed in Kamloops, British Columbia, and our hearts were all heavy. We said a prayer for those who did not survive and in a moment of joy amid grief, she and her sisters sang us "You Are My Sunshine" in Kwak'wala. Watching my aunties sing and dance in Alert Bay, I was so moved that I had to turn off my camera to hide my tears. It felt like I was right there with them, and at the same time, I felt so far away. My heart ached for this community that felt like home but that I had visited only once before.

When I told my grandfather what had happened, he talked to me about his connection to that place. "It's where I was born," he said. Alert Bay's hospital was the nearest one to Blunden Harbour, his home community, where he grew up speaking Kwak'wala until he was a teenager. That's when he went back to Alert Bay, to attend residential school at St. Michael's. This I already knew, even though he never spoke about it other than to say that he went there to learn English.

I didn't want to pry by asking for more than what he shared freely, so I left it there and kept searching for answers in my own way. I became somewhat of a family archivist, poring over newspapers and collecting screenshots of articles that mentioned our family's art and history of political resistance in defence of our cultural heritage.

I read in an interview with my grandfather that Alert Bay is also where the love of my family began: my grandmother caught his eye as she was leaving the ferry. They fell in love and moved to the mainland to start a family, but it was there, on the shores of that little island, that I became a possibility because two people fell in love.

After such a moving language lesson, I continued to follow the cultural centre and other related accounts online, and eventually enrolled in a program blending yoga, Kwakiutl cultural teachings, Kwak'wala language instruction, and culturally appropriate health and wellness information. My newfound auntie was our elder, and for weeks I learned from her and other instructors. A cousin of mine, whom I also met through the language class, was in the program, too. With each lesson, I was connecting to home, at least virtually, watching my auntie and other instructors who lived there smiling at me onscreen. I was learning new words, sounding them out tentatively while savouring the accomplishment of my growing vocabulary. I completed the program, and it was time to graduate.

When I first read about the program, there was talk about a graduation ceremony in Alert Bay, but I doubted it would happen, given the ever-changing public health orders. Still, I hoped against hope it would actually come to pass; that I would find my way back home. Fortune was on our side.

On the morning of the graduation, I went to the cultural centre, where a photo of my grandfather and great-great grandfather hung on the wall. I took in my family's artwork before finally making my way to the Big House, the building that serves as the spiritual and cultural centre of the community.

There were glorious speeches, a fire in the centre, and a big spread of food that smelled so heavenly. I thought about how hungry I was all the time when I first saw Alert Bay hanging on the wall of my hospital room during my eating disorder treatment, and now here I was, feasting with my family. My team of specialists were afraid for me to exercise, and now I am teaching yoga.

We were ushered into the back to prepare for a Ladies Dance. I had never been taught to dance traditionally, except once as a child at a cousin's wedding, and I worried I'd look silly. Wrapped in a borrowed shawl, I joined the other ladies in my program and learned the dance.

As I walked out onto the Big House floor, my toes connected with the cool earth, and I remembered how cold, sterile, and unyielding the hospital floor was. I felt unsteady and tentative, not from the dizziness, but inexperience; my auntie took me by the hand and showed me what to do.

I let the earth stick to the soles of my feet, the dirt get between my toes, guided across the floor by my relative. I felt grounded, even though I was very much in motion, both in body and heart, walking tall as a Kwakwaka'wakw woman. I was so moved to be in the Big House, dancing on the land where my grandpa was born, where my grandparents fell in love, where our family's carvings stand tall.

DIMITRI NASRALLAH

Crybaby

In November 2009, I returned to Lebanon for the first time since we boarded a ferry and sailed off to Cyprus that fateful morning when I was five. Though we'd left as a family twenty-seven years ago, I was returning alone. It felt like something I had to do, that I couldn't put off any longer.

I remember the trepidation of the flight to Beirut, its long stopover in Paris, of leaving Montreal and my wife at the time, at the beginning of her second trimester, to spend a month in a place I only knew from the furthest reaches of my memory. I was writing a second novel, and I was failing at it, unable to find its core after multiple drafts. It had transformed into a story about leaving Lebanon, but it had no beating heart. Lebanon was a world that I knew, but from which I was inherently distanced. I had anger in my life because of it, frustrations at being pulled across the world and uprooted many times with what felt like arbitrary strictness. When I was young, I planted all that anger on my parents. But now that I had lived alone for a few years, there was no way to leave all those memories behind. I did not want to pass on those reverberations to the child due next April.

There weren't many passengers on the turbulent Middle East Airlines flight from Paris to Beirut. As the plane approached the airport and the Mediterranean below finally gave way to the shores of Lebanon, I was able to move into a window seat and take in every moment of the descent. I had come back for answers, but I didn't know what questions I was asking, and so I wanted to absorb everything—the shoreline oil refineries, the unfinished buildings everywhere, the yellow cloud that hung over the city in the air. I knew a fair bit of trivia about the land below. Ever since the assassination of Prime Minister Rafic Hariri in 2005, followed by the war with Israel in 2006, I had awakened to the fact that I could read Lebanon's daily news online. I had read about the country's ongoing struggle to distance itself from Syrian influence, Israeli aggression, the growing power base for Hezbollah's political arm among Shiites, the regular assassinations of public intellectuals. I knew that the same political families who'd been in power when I left at age five were still in power as I returned at age thirty-two.

What I did not know as well, and which was much more intimidating, was the large, multibranched family I had there. After I had retrieved my suitcase, I walked out into the arrivals area and looked around for my Uncle Murad and Aunt Muna, my mother's brother and his wife, whom I fondly remembered as having visited us in Athens and Toronto, where I'd spent my childhood. Their youngest son, Raja, had been my best friend when I lived in Beirut. Their oldest son, Eid, had died at eleven years old, the victim of a car bomb that had gone off on a street near their apartment building.

I looked around the arrivals area for my uncle's thick glasses, my aunt's straight brown hair, but they found me first. "Keefak, ya sabeh?" Uncle Murad said as he pulled me in for a hug.

"How you've grown!" my aunt Muna exclaimed, kissing my cheeks.

I was immediately transported back to when I was young and my uncle would give me loose change for candy, and my aunt would wet the ends of a tissue to clean my cheek at church. Maybe it was because I was exhausted from travel, but their warmth was sudden and unexpected, an affection from loving adults that I hadn't even realized I'd been miss-ing all along. It wasn't the culture that was cold, distracted, and distant—it was just my parents.

We drove through the south ends of the city toward their home in Hamra, near the American University in the commercial heart of Ras Beirut, an area that saw some of the fiercest battles of the civil war back when we lived there. I exchanged news of my family as I looked out the window at the bustling, chaotic driving around my uncle's car, the brown dirt that made up the sides of the roads, the new construction sites going up next to bullet-marked abandoned buildings awaiting demolition, and I thought again of how I had initiated this trip in secret, without telling my parents. Having joined Facebook the year before, I'd connected with my relatives on my own for the first time. I'd previously shunned rela-tives or anything to do with family. Our first decade in Canada had been tumultuous and filled with sacrifice, and I'd concluded that I was better off alone, reinventing myself without family or the heritage attached to them. But now that I was an adult preparing to have his own child, I began to see them differently. I'd written to my aunt and expressed my interest in visiting Lebanon. To my surprise, she wrote back within the hour inviting me to stay with them for as long as I liked.

In the car, she turned around and said to me, "Everyone is so curious to meet you. We've even had calls from your dad's side of the family."

"How do they even know I'm here?" My father was the youngest of eight brothers and sisters, who each had gone on to have their own large families, and since they were all mostly a generation older, I knew few of my many paternal cousins.

"The news spreads," she said. "Everyone wants to know what happened."

"What do you mean?"

"Your family is the only one that has never returned," my uncle said, his eyes on the road. "They erased us all from their lives."

"Everyone else came back?"

"Everyone but your mother and father."

"It hasn't been easy for them," I said, feeling obliged to defend my parents. Here, I quickly realized, I was not my own person, but an extension of them. "We live halfway around the world."

"Sure, you're right," my uncle said. "But even when they were young, they couldn't leave quick enough."

In Beirut, in between daily meetings with relatives, I walked a lot. I walked along Hamra Street and looked at all the shops. I walked along the Corniche and stared out at the sea. I walked along Bliss Street and tried to remember what it all looked like when I was last here, when it was falling apart, just boarded-up storefronts among those that hadn't yet been cratered. Where before you wouldn't see a student outside the American University's gates, there were now crowds of students loafing around at the tables of small cafés. I walked around for hours, cataloguing everything I saw and heard and smelled, because it felt so precarious to even be here, against my parents' wishes, in this land that they know so much better but had absolutely no interest in seeing again.

I spent time with my aunt Souad, my mother's older sister. She looked like my mother, but spoke more generously and smiled more frequently. We sat in her small living room, in a room where I remember my uncle used to keep a barbershop during the war. My aunt Muna had come along as my mediator, because we all sensed it was a strange experience to reconnect with relatives you should know but don't.

"You used to spend a lot of time here," Aunt Souad said in Arabic, the only language she speaks. "Every day you were here, when Maha went to work."

"I remember spending time with Roula," I said of her daughter, who was about seven or eight years older than me. This was the most Arabic I'd used since I was eleven and we'd moved to Canada. Even though I could still understand it fluently, I'd lost my ability to write and read it, and only had a child's portion of the spoken language from when my parents would sometimes speak it at home.

"Roula looked after you. We raised you as one of our own. It's so good to see you again."

My aunt was seated across from me with her hands folded, a tray of baklava and bitter coffee between us, my other aunt in an armchair to the side, remembering vividly what once happened in this room, recollections of which I only had scant details.

"I lived upstairs," I finally said, to say something at all.

"That's right. Two floors up, the fourth. It was your father's apartment. Keefo Camille?"

"My dad? He's fine."

"You know, I introduced them. Camille knew my Eli, back when he was alive, bless his soul." My uncle had died of a heart attack several years back. "He lived upstairs."

"Your mother lived with Murad and me," Aunt Muna said. "Before that she lived alone with Jidduh."

"Why did she move in with you?"

"To go to school," Aunt Muna said. "Besides, it wasn't easy to live with Jidduh in a small village like Marjeyoun after her mother died. He drank too much. She couldn't take care of him on her own. So they both came to live with us. She was too intelligent to want to stay down in the village, where there's nothing."

"Maha was so young when that happened, I remember," Aunt Souad said. "The rest of us, we were older, but Maha was still a teenager. She was with our mother when she had her stroke. She was the one who saw her die."

"We all helped her a lot," Aunt Muna said. "You came down here and stayed with Souad every day when she went to work. It was me in the end who looked after her father."

"It would be so nice if she came to visit us," my aunt Souad said. "Tell her we miss her, and that I'm too old to travel."

"I'll tell her," I said. I looked around the room, out the window. "Everywhere I see things that look familiar. I think about our apartment upstairs a lot," I confessed.

"It's empty now," Aunt Souad said. "You want to see it?"

We crowded into the elevator, and went down to the landing, where my aunt spoke with the concierge, who eyed me suspiciously. It turned out he still remembered my father. Why anyone would feel nostalgic about that apartment, he couldn't understand, but he relented in the end and took us up. We stepped into one of the smallest apartments I'd ever seen, smaller even than our first apartment in Montreal. The tiny bathroom had a shower head inches away from the toilet that pointed directly upon a drain in the floor. The kitchen was the size of a closet, another feature the apartment did not have. Its only saving grace was the balcony overlooking the university and then the sea. I tried to imagine the shag carpet, white shelving, and dark-brown sofa of our old living room. I remember my father had a record player, with a small collection of records he kept up high and with which I was fascinated. I could not imagine how my parents had fit a double bed and a bunk bed in the bedroom. I remembered falling off that bunk headfirst one time. Where would I have even had room to land? I wondered.

"I remember this all being so much bigger," I said.

"You were smaller," Aunt Muna said.

"I remember being so happy here."

"Really? We were all so worried for you. You were a crybaby. Any little sound or fall would send you to tears. Your mother would get so fed up, it happened so much."

That afternoon, I walked down the Corniche to the city's deserted public beach. People here would much rather pay to access the hotel waterfronts or beach clubs instead. The public beach was visited by a few Shiites, who would remain draped in robes and wade into the shoreline only ankle-deep, or Syrian teens washing up after working construction jobs.

I took off my shirt, set my phone deep in my shoe, and walked along the shore, acclimating to the lazy waves as they lapped at my shins. I waded in farther, dove in gently, and swam out a few metres, then settled on my back and floated for as long as the air in my lungs would keep me up. From this vantage point, I had my favourite view of the city, the version of Beirut I wanted to commit to memory.

All of the other portraits were claustrophobic. It was a city teeming upon itself: fashionistas sidestepping past beggars, refugee kids playing in the rocks beneath million-dollar condos owned by Saudi vacationers, new buildings growing like weeds out of the rubble of buildings abandoned, the leftovers of war still swept to the backs of vacant lots or the sides of highways. But floating on my back in the sea, I could push away from it all and see the city as a tapestry of rushing cars, palm trees, skylines of glass and metal and cinder block, young mothers pushing strollers along the boardwalk, delivery trucks parked across the street, the almost perennially blue sky.

I thought back to what my aunt had said: that I'd been an anxious child, a crybaby, needy. I'd never remembered myself that way, though to think of it now, lying in the sea and staring at the city, I did wet my bed till the age of twelve. How much of that had to do with the war? With shuttering ourselves indoors for safety, running down staircases, panicking at the sudden shake of nearby bombing, being pulled by the collar to run away? How could I not act fearful, with fear all around me? It must have found a way in.

I remembered being a happy child in Greece, up until that all changed and my father moved away, and then we immigrated to Canada. I remember being frustrated with my lot in life once we got to

Canada, feeling my angriest. I blamed my parents for that, but mostly my mom, because my dad wasn't engaged with us enough to notice my anger. But what if that anger had been an echo of what had first happened here? What if part of the venom was fomenting from this life before memories were formed, when I was in the hands of people who had their own lives and troubles before the war even began?

I swam back to shore, baptized by realization, as if seeing the constellation of events that made up my life; the one extra detail about my neediness had finally revealed to me the person I really was.

I went back to swim in the sea every day for the rest of that week. It reminded me of all the times my father had brought us swimming at the beach club not far away when we lived just up the street. By week's end, I got sick and lost my appetite. My skin grew pale and my cheeks gaunt, as I slept all day, too weak to move.

My aunt Muna came to feel my head with the back of her hand. "You shouldn't have gone swimming in the sea," she said. "That water's polluted."

ESMERALDA CABRAL

Such a Pity, Senhora

I had my ears pierced when I was three weeks old. Not that I remember, but my mother talked about this often, and offered it as an explanation for my fascination with earrings from a young age. Apparently, when I was two years old, I asked Santa for a pair of earrings, and I squealed with delight when I opened my gift on Christmas Eve. That whole scene has become part of our family lore.

When I arrived in Canada at the age of seven, I learned that not all girls got their ears pierced as babies. Many of my friends in elementary school told me their parents wouldn't allow them to get their ears pierced at all, even in Grade 5 or 6.

"Huh," I used to say. "Why not?"

When my daughter was born, though, my Canadian husband and I decided that we would not inflict this Portuguese cultural tradition on her. Instead, we would wait until she voiced her own desire to have her ears pierced. I sensed my mother was disappointed, but she didn't say much. "Can I give her a gold chain, then?" she asked.

"Sure, we'll keep it for when she's older, though," I said. "Because I think it's kind of dangerous. I mean, what if it catches on something and she chokes?"

20

My mother reminded me that my sisters and I had all worn gold chains from the day we were born, and we had never choked, but "it's up to you," she said. "I don't want to be responsible if anything happens."

These traditions involving jewellery seemed trivial to me. What I thought was important was for my children to grow up with a strong sense of their Portuguese heritage. I felt we could foster this by taking them to Portugal early in their lives, and then as often as possible. That way they could learn the cultural norms in the proper context, I reasoned. My husband agreed.

On his first sabbatical leave as a university professor, Eric decided he would conduct research in New Zealand, so our family moved there for most of the year. Afterward, he would be writing scientific papers based on that research, and he could do that from anywhere. "Why don't we go to Portugal?" he offered.

We decided to spend three months on my home island of São Miguel, in the Azores, the Portuguese archipelago of nine islands located in the Mid-Atlantic. It would give us an opportunity to reacquaint ourselves with the island, and also to introduce the children, young as they were, to Portuguese culture.

Our son, Matt, was five years old, and baby Georgia was eight months and not yet walking. We found it easy to travel with the children at this age. Georgia was still mostly breastfeeding, and Matt was readily entertained by rocks and sticks and sandy beaches.

We stood out as foreigners. We wore hats and sunglasses, and we carried Georgia in a backpack. People often stopped and unabashedly stared at us. The baby carrier was a great conversation starter—I often ended up chatting on the street, in Portuguese, to people I didn't know, my accent revealing that I am an islander, like them.

One day, Eric was at home writing, and I decided to take the children to the piscina, a natural rocky seaside pool, for a swim. I stopped for a coffee on the way, and, while I was in the queue, a woman struck up a conversation with me. She fussed over the children, mostly Georgia, and said how beautiful she was, those cheeks, those eyes. She kissed her face, and then bent down and gave Matt a lollipop.

I wasn't thrilled about the candy, or the kiss, but I knew she was trying to be kind. I smiled and said obrigada, then quickly finished my coffee and rushed back out into the sun with the children, and down the hill to the seashore. I felt a strange sensation on the top of my head, but I shrugged it off and thought it was likely due to fatigue or the intense heat. Once I got to the pool and changed into my bathing suit, I put my hand to my head and felt a lollipop stuck to my hair! I had to get the lifeguard to cut it off, and a chunk of my hair, too.

"Why didn't you tell me the lady had given one to Georgia, too?" I asked Matt.

My horror at seeing the tuft of short hair on top of my head was compounded when I thought of my baby, barely eating solids, sucking on a lollipop. I don't remember what I said, but I was near tears. I can still hear the lifeguard saying, "Oh, senhora, it's only sugar."

Giving sweets, I learned, was one way that adults showed kindness to young children. I had already noticed that children were highly prized in island culture. Whenever we went out for dinner, families sat together, sometimes with toddlers and babies who were remarkably well-behaved. If a baby cried, there were no hostile looks from other patrons for the ambiance being ruined; rather, people showed concern and offered to hold the children or even entertain them while their parents finished their dinner.

I had left the island as a child and immigrated to Canada with my parents, but our ties to the Azores remained strong, and we visited often. I could speak the language well, and I found it easy to reinsert myself into island life whenever I returned. I had always gone back for short visits, though, and this would be, by far, the longest time I had spent there since immigrating.

I was aware that it was a class-oriented society, that people tend to mingle primarily within their social class—professionals don't really mix with fishers and labourers, for example. But I had grown up mostly in Canada, where society seemed more egalitarian, and I was uncomfortable with elitism. This was one part of my culture that I didn't care for, and I had decided even before arriving that I wouldn't buy into the whole class thing—I would talk to everyone, just as I did in Canada.

We rented a house in a village adjacent to the one where my family was from. It was a short uphill walk from the house where we had lived, but it might as well have been on the other side of the archipelago. I didn't know anyone who lived there. I knew we would be the foreigners, coming to live in this small place, and word would get around that we were from North America.

That summer was one of the hottest on record. Our rental was in the middle of a row of attached houses perched on a cliff top, overlooking fields of grapes and vegetables, and the Atlantic Ocean beyond. When I hung the laundry on the line on the back deck, I could gaze to the horizon and imagine life beyond that line. On a map, I could see that there was no land directly to the south, between us and Antarctica. Sometimes I'd sit out on the patio and let the hot sun bake my skin, but I never lasted very long. Instead, I spent most days at the beach or the seashore with the children, where the breeze from the water kept us cool. Eric found it hard to work in the heat and eventually started writing in the early mornings and evenings only, which freed him during the day to accompany us on our adventures.

The town became livelier after sunset. I noticed that after dinner, the women on the street would sit on their front stoops or lean out their windows to watch the goings-on and chat with each other. Their husbands would go to the local coffee shops or bars to meet with friends.

After a week or two of witnessing this, I was brave enough to sit out on my front stoop as well. I knew I'd be disrupting the habitual, but I welcomed the opportunity to speak my language and to get to know my neighbours. I would sit out there with Georgia while Eric read to Matt and put him to bed. Then I'd go inside and start the process with the baby.

During the day, we'd often meet friends at the piscina. I told one of them that I had this evening ritual with the neighbourhood women and my friend sounded surprised.

"What do you have in common with them? What do you talk about?" she asked.

"Ha, lots, actually. Mostly we talk about the kids. Sometimes they ask questions about Canada. They keep calling Eric an Americano and I have to remind them that he's Canadian," I explained.

"Oh, don't bother, it's all the same to us," my friend said with a grin.

One evening, I was feeling especially tired, and opted out of the chat-fest. The kids were cranky, and I thought we could all benefit from an early night. As I was nursing Georgia to sleep, I could hear the women coming onto the street, talking and laughing. I had closed the bedroom shutters, but the windows were open, and I could hear them clearly.

"She's so friendly. She talks to everyone," I heard my next-door neighbour say.

"Her husband doesn't say much, though." I think that was the neighbour from across the street and down a house or two.

"He doesn't speak Portuguese!" another woman said, sounding like she was defending Eric.

"They say he's a professor, but have you seen the way he dresses? Sandals and shorts! What kind of professor dresses like that?"

"And that poor baby. She doesn't even have shoes. And the little boy—so shy…"

I couldn't identify some of the voices.

"Have you noticed the little girl doesn't have her ears pierced?"

"I've heard that's not the style in America."

"But she's Portuguese!" My neighbour was sounding passionate.

I felt like I was intruding on a private conversation and got up to close the window.

The next evening, I joined in again. Someone said it was nice to see me out there, that they'd missed me. I explained that we had all felt tired the day before, too much sun, maybe, so we'd put the kids to bed early and I had let myself fall asleep.

"But you know, the windows were open, and I could hear you out here. You know that I can understand everything you say, don't you?"

They didn't seem fazed or apologetic. We just kept talking as if last evening's conversation had not been awkward at all.

"Tell me, vizinha," one woman asked me, "why does that beautiful baby of yours not have her ears pierced? Is it because your husband doesn't like our ways?"

"Oh, no," I chuckled. "That's not it at all. We've just agreed that we will let her decide for herself and she can get it done when she wants to."

"Such a pity," she said.

I became very fond of these women. So much so that as our departure neared, I felt an impending sense of loss. I was going to miss them. One morning, as I was contemplating just that, I heard a knock on the door. When I answered, there stood one of the women from farther down the street, one whom I didn't know very well, but recognized right away. She held an envelope in her hand.

"Bom dia, please, please come in," I said.

"Just for a minute, senhora." She stepped inside so I could close the door and shut out the traffic noise.

She handed me the envelope and said, "This is for you. From all of us."

"Oh, thank you! What is it?"

I opened the envelope and saw that there was money inside.

"There's enough there for you to get your baby's ears pierced. We think that maybe your husband won't give you the money to have it done because he doesn't like it, so we all pitched in a little bit for you."

"Oh, senhora! Obrigada." I felt the tears rush to my eyes. "What a lovely thing to do."

"We all really like you, and we're so sad that you're going back to America." She said this as she bit her bottom lip and turned her face away.

"To Canada. And we'll be back, you know," I said.

I kept in touch by mail with some of the neighbours for a few years. Usually at Christmas. Our family did go back to Portugal several times after that, but mostly we went to the mainland. We made short side trips to São Miguel, but packed them with sightseeing and visits to family. It was fifteen years before we made it back to that same town. We walked the cobblestoned streets and climbed the hill to feast our eyes on that glorious view again. Snippets of memories came back to Matt, but Georgia looked at it all as if for the first time, of course.

I knocked on the door of the next-door neighbour's house. A young woman answered, someone we didn't recognize.

"Oh, we're looking for Senhora Olivia," I said.

"That's my mother," she said. "I live here with her now after my father passed away."

When I explained who we were, she said she knew of us, and was very happy to meet us. She invited us in, but cautioned that her mother might not recognize us. "She is having trouble remembering some things these days," she said. And then she continued, "You probably know that the neighbour across the street from those days moved to Boston, and the one who lived upstairs from her has moved to the city."

"No, I didn't know," I said.

We walked down a dark hallway to the back of the house. Senhora Olivia was sitting at a table on the deck, sipping from a cup of tea. We greeted her then joined her for tea. I showed pictures from when we had last lived there, but wondered if she remembered us. I put my arm around my daughter and said, "And this is baby Georgia. And look, she got her ears pierced!" Georgia turned her head to the side to show off her traditional gold hoops. She bought into the tradition on her own accord, at the age of six.

Senhora Olivia gave Georgia a broad smile. Then she looked at each of us in turn and her eyes welled up. I like to think that at that precise moment, she knew exactly who we were.

KATHRYN GWUN-YEEN LENNON

Ah-Ling Ge Lui Fan Lai La! Ah-Ling's Girl Has Come Home

2018

The smell of brine fills my nose as the ferry pulls up to the 長洲 Cheung Chau pier. A sailor in a navy blue uniform with white trim tosses a mooring rope around a dock bollard and brings us in. I disembark, heavy-legged from a trans-Pacific red-eye flight and fifteen-hour time difference. Push through a crowd of people in business attire and school uniforms boarding the ferry for its next sailing back to Hong Kong Island.

My feet know the way from here. They carry me straight up through the plaza, right at the dim sum restaurant, down past the housewares shop and hairdresser, and around the corner. I stop to wave at the neighbour smoking cigarettes and hanging her laundry, then reach over the waist-high, brown metal gate and let myself in. But this time, I don't know what to expect. Pau Pau, my maternal grandmother, passed away four days ago, and I'm here with my parents and sister for the funeral.

My mother, Ah-Ling, was born on a tombolo named 長洲 Cheung Chau, literally "long island," one of Hong Kong's 263 outlying islands. The majority of Cheung Chau's seventy thousand inhabitants live elbow-to-elbow on the flat part of the island, between two rocky hills at the northern and southern ends. Three-storey walk-up apartments are so close to each other that you can watch your neighbour's TV. Laundry flaps on rooftops. Sampans and fishing boats jostle in the harbour. The outdoor seaside restaurants are popular weekend destinations for local tourists. Save for specially designed miniature ambulances and fire trucks, no cars are allowed on the island; the streets are too narrow and crowded with people: Indonesian and Filipina domestic helpers pushing grandparents in wheelchairs; weekend tourists careening on rented bikes; dock workers hauling all manner of goods on rackety dollies. The island is known for its street snacks (especially fish balls), and as home to the treasure cave of nineteenth-century pirate Cheung Po Tsai. My grandfather, Gong Gong, was born on the island into a farming family. Pau Pau was urban, born into a family of steelworkers on Hong Kong Island, the centre of the British colony, in a district called Sai Ying Poon, once a fishing port and the British military's first base.

On one visit back to Hong Kong for a cousin's wedding, my sister and I went to Sai Ying Poon looking for Pau Pau's childhood home. We arrived at the address given to us by our uncle to be greeted by the blocky indifference of a sleek luxury apartment. How naive of us to think we might find some fragment of connection to an ancestral home that had twice been replaced. Later, we sat at a bar overlooking the street sipping on a beer called gwai lo (literally foreign devil, meaning foreigner or white guy). On another visit, a few months later, a friend and I stumbled upon Tuck Chong Sum Kee Bamboo Steamer Company, a shop making bamboo steamers the traditional way. Stepping inside, we watched the maker work, tucked between steamers stacked up to the ceiling. He used his bare feet to hold one end of a piece of bamboo while he wrapped the other end around a frame. Some of them were stamped with the name NEWTOWN BAKERY, a Chinese Filipino bakery and restaurant I'd eaten at countless times in Vancouver's Chinatown. A place where I'd shared conversations with other diasporic friends about Hong Kong, our grandparents, cultural identity, the future of Chinatowns. Ten thousand kilometres of distance and differences were knotted together in an unexpected moment of connection.

I've made the journey at regular intervals throughout my life. Sometimes with family, sometimes with friends, sometimes solo. Growing up in a middle-class, semi-diasporic family, we travelled internationally only to visit the homeland. No Disneyland or Caribbean resorts. It was either road trips, motels, and car-camping in Western Canada or a fourteen-hour overseas flight to one of the most densely populated cities in the world. When we would visit Hong Kong on summer holidays, our home base was always Pau Pau's house on Cheung Chau.

The first time we visited, I was five years old and my sister was one, plane tickets came in special envelopes, and meals came with silverware. I remember being embraced by clouds of diesel and the smell of hot garbage as we stepped out of a taxi at Central Ferry Piers on Hong Kong Island, lemon tea and instant cup noodles on the ferry to Cheung Chau, the narrow streets of my mother's birthplace.

My Canadian-born senses had no point of comparison for the whole pigs hanging by their snouts in the open storefronts of butchers. But I was enthralled with the shops bursting with bright plastic beach toys and the latest Twin Stars and Hello Kitty stationery. In every photo, my chubby cheeks flush, bangs stick to my sweaty forehead, and I tower above my Hong Kong cousins. I don't know if it was to save dishwashing water or a subtle way of showing care, but Pau Pau always had a designated mug for each of us in her living-room drawer. We were not to drink out of anyone else's.

2018

My family is out for a hike around the island's mini Great Wall. It's been ten days since I last washed my hair, and my scalp itches in the mid-morning sun. My mother, sister, and I are observing a Chinese custom where you stop washing your hair from the day someone passes away until their funeral rites are completed. For the last ten days we've been folding gold and silver paper into ingots, to burn as offerings at Pau Pau's funeral. My great-aunt drops by every day to check in on us, popping over from the corner store she owns and lives above down the street. Other than that, there have been no visiting relatives, no sight-seeing, no shopping. So instead, we're out for a hike. The sky is a brilliant blue. There are no swimmers in the water today. We see the aftermath of Typhoon Mangkhut: streetlights tilted at jarring angles, the paved road leading to the helipad is twisted metal and broken concrete. Had the road not been twisted up, this is where Pau Pau would have been transferred out of the ambulance to be flown to the bigger hospital on Hong Kong Island. They had to drive her to a sports field to catch the helicopter.

I always assumed my Pau Pau never saw me as Chinese. With my barely passable Cantonese, my mixed-raceness, my gwai lo father, my Canadian upbringing.

My first-generation Hong Kong immigrant mother and fifth-generation Irish-Canadian settler father didn't know how to raise us to talk about race. Nor were we raised to really think of ourselves as Chinese. I've often wished I could be better at thickening my skin to the mixed messages I've internalized about my identity. In elementary school, I couldn't keep up with my Cantonese-speaking classmates on the playground. Yet I'd go to after-school Chinese calligraphy class and Chinese summer camps, and most of our meals out were in Edmonton's Chinese and Chinatown restaurants. As an adult, many a white stranger felt compelled to tell me about their Asian wife or trip to China, before learning anything else about me. Chinese relatives sometimes still ask if I can use chopsticks. Sinophiles have boasted to me about how many Chinese characters they've memorized, and expressed surprise that I have far fewer in my repertoire. Fellow Chinese diasporic friends have let me know that I'm not *really* Chinese because my parents didn't keep their extra garbage bags in the dishwasher, or don't know the difference between how to pronounce mustard (gaai laat) and greens (gaai laan). As an adult, I've had white colleagues in a workplace lunchroom wrinkle their nose at my tofu.

2011

When I was in my mid-twenties and had just finished my undergrad, I decided to take my savings and journey "back" to the motherland. I thought it would be a way of rooting myself, to find my way out of the cloud of identity confusion and discomfort in my own skin that had been my experience as a mixed-race Asian woman. To help me self-locate in relation to living in settler-colonial Canada, the place I called home, as a non-white settler, whose ancestors had migrated here from other British colonies. I bought a one-way plane ticket to Hong Kong, and made a loose plan. I'd live with Pau Pau for a while, learn more Cantonese and Mandarin, maybe find a job, maybe volunteer on an organic farm, and in doing so, voilà! I would become more Chinese. My mother arranged that I would pay Pau Pau a small amount each month for "electricity." I hung out for a few months and overstayed my welcome. I thought I had designed a self-directed, study-abroad session where I would learn from my elders, connect with my roots, and reclaim my culture and language. Instead, it was an awkward, fumbling time, filled with conflict. I was scolded for the way I did laundry (not frequently enough), for the way I once rested my chopsticks on my bowl (upright is offensive), for hanging out with boys. Almost daily, Pau Pau would ask, "Why are you here?"

One month into my sojourn, with Lunar New Year approaching, Pau Pau handed me a lycee, a red envelope stuffed with several crisp Hong Kong banknotes. She shooed me out of the house, urging me to go haang gaai 行街—to go window shopping/to go for a walk—to buy new clothes for the new year. I wandered down the street to one of the boutiques and picked out a cozy navy blue sweater with white polka dots and a row of buttons down the back. I got home and pulled it out of its crinkly pink plastic bag, proud to show her. I'm doing it! Living my culture!

Her face fell and she sighed loudly, "Ai ya!"

I had no idea what was going on. She picked up the phone and jabbed in the fourteen digits of a long-distance number, muttering, "Your mother didn't teach you anything."

"Wai?" My mom's sleepy voice answered. It was midnight in Edmonton.

Pau Pau spoke rapidly to my mom, intermittently waving her crooked finger at me, then handed me the phone.

My mom explained, "For Chinese New Year, you need to wear lucky colours—red, pink, even purple would be okay. But you chose the most unlucky colours. Blue and white. Those are funeral colours." I couldn't have done any worse.

Pau Pau got her change purse, her umbrella. We were going out. She marched me down the street to another boutique and jabbed her umbrella at the entrance, telling me to go in. I stepped in through a heavy plastic curtain, and my eyes landed on a bright red sweatshirt jacket. I tried it on, and the sleeves came halfway up my forearm—I was pretty sure it was not meant to be three-quarter sleeves, but it was unlikely I'd find anything at the little island shops that fit my (relatively gigantic and broad-shouldered) Canadian frame. I glanced up, looking for Pau Pau. She nodded her gruff approval. Good enough. *Oh well, I'll just roll them up.* I bought the sweatshirt. We walked around the corner to her favourite wonton place for a quick, affordable dinner of steaming wonton mein. All in all, a successful outing.

On the way home, we passed balconies illuminated by firelight; those who still observed the traditions were burning paper money in red tins to welcome the new year. We bumped into a neighbour pushing a little dog in a shopping cart. We exchanged red envelopes, "Sun tay gin hong!"—wishing you health and happiness. The dog put its paws together to wish us a happy New Year.

2018

The night before Pau Pau's funeral, we can't sleep in the eerie emptiness of her apartment and so my sister, my father, and I walk with my mother to one of the island's plazas. There, inside of a large white funeral tent that has been set up for the multi-day funeral rites, we sit for the final 2:00 a.m. to 5:00 a.m. shift of the wake: an overnight vigil to ensure that Pau Pau has a smooth journey into the afterlife. The tent is open on the side facing the plaza. A wooden coffin and a framed photo of Pau Pau sit at one end. A pack of dogs runs by, howling in the cold. We sit with my cousins, huddled around a fire in a red tin bucket, feeding gold and silver joss paper squares and paper bills into the fire, one by one, to make sure she has enough money for the journey ahead.

When the sky starts to lighten, someone delivers hot tea and dim sum to us, and we eat together at a round table at the far end of the tent. We head back to the apartment to dress from head to foot in white for the funeral. Our Christian family members dress in black. The girls pin blue crocheted flowers in our hair. We gather back at the tent to observe the traditions my grandmother lived strictly by: we bai sun 拜神. We pay our respects, honour the ancestors, and honour the gods by offering incense and prayers. In the plaza, we burn cardboard and paper versions of all the items she'll need to be comfortable in the afterlife: a car, clothing, a watch, money, and even a life-size mah-jong table. We form a procession and wind slowly up the steep hillside to the crematorium.

2008

On one visit, before arthritis made it difficult for her to walk, I filmed Pau Pau's whole morning routine. We had a 7:30 a.m. start: dim sum at her favourite restaurant, then a stop at her regular newsstand to pick up the newspaper and a packet of tissues. A second stop at the public wet market to buy fish and veggies for lunch. Then home to read the newspaper while her domestic helper, Missy, prepared lunch.

Along the way, she ran into friends and acquaintances. Some of them said they'd noticed me walking around the island and wondered who this foreigner was. When Pau Pau explained that I was her granddaughter, they exclaimed, "Wah! Ah-Ling ge lui fan lai la!" Ah-Ling's girl has come home.

And she just beamed.

2011

If I planned to go into Hong Kong for a day of exploring or visiting cousins, Pau Pau would ask, "Lai maya fun jong dap shun fan lay?" What time are you taking the ferry to come back?

I would pull out her pocket-sized ferry schedule from its spot beside her land line, and wobble through the Cantonese numbers on my fingers, yat-yee-sam-say-mm-look-tzat-but-gau to land on gau. "Gau deem dap shun." The 9:00 p.m. big ferry.

Over my many visits, I've come to prefer the big ferry. It's slower, and takes an hour to get from Hong Kong Island to Cheung Chau. I love sitting in the last row of seats on the open-air deck at the back of the boat. Sipping on syrupy lemon tea from the onboard vending machine. Watching the tiara of Hong Kong's lights soften into the distance as the boat slips back through the slick black water.

In my late teens and early twenties, as a fresh backpacker, I thought I knew how to travel. To travel was to pack a backpack with a guidebook and the essentials, to pass through new places, navigate the unknown, gather experiences, and return home changed by it all. Maybe it seems obvious to say, but I wonder now if my trips to Hong Kong were more about visiting. My map of Cheung Chau and Hong Kong is woven from threads of memories and experiences. Travelling and visiting overlap. To visit is to be picked up at the airport, to bring oranges, to be offered cold lemon tea. To be a good guest, to be accountable, to maintain relationships.

2018

Because Pau Pau lived past ninety, they call it a 笑喪 smiling funeral. After the funeral, the sky lights up. In the final funeral rite, we are the last to jump over the fire and splash our faces with pomelo leaf water. We wash our hair, and switch the blue flowers for red ones. My sister and I put on newly purchased, loudly colourful clothes. Today, the ugly duckling self-consciousness I usually feel about being the sweaty, clumsy Canadian among my matte, sleek Hong Kong cousins is nowhere to be found. I proudly wear my red floral shirt and forest green pants to the hotel lunch that marks the end of my Pau Pau's funeral festivities, knowing she would approve.

I imagine her standing on her ground-floor balcony, waving "bye-bye" and miming putting on a backpack, saying, "Fong ga fan lai la." Come back when you have holidays. Then waving us off with a final "joy geen" or "bye-bye."

I wonder, if I visit now, will my feet still take me to her house? Who will be sitting by the open door in the rattan chair, ankles crossed, one eye scanning for neighbourhood gossip? Will they set down their newspaper? Will they extend a gnarled hand to accept the bag of oranges I offer them? Roll the fruit into a bowl, then smooth out the translucent red plastic bag, fold it neatly, and place it in the drawer under the land line? Will they take out my mug and offer me some boiled water 滾水 gwan seoi?

I didn't know then that Pau Pau's funeral would be my last trip to Hong Kong before three major events would rock the city, the world, and my life dramatically: the Hong Kong protests, COVID-19, and becoming a mother. Since then, I've procrastinated finishing a poetry project that delves into my relationship with the Cantonese language. I've felt like an imposter formulating an opinion about the Hong Kong protests. I haven't found time to reflect on what her journey from this world means for my loosening ties to my mother's motherland. I've lost my sense of urgency to learn the language. I am less sure of my right, ability, or desire to lay any kind of claim to a Chinese, Cantonese, or Hong Konger identity. And I wonder if im/migration is not a one-way journey but an oscillation. A shuttle on a loom. A portal opened between worlds for a shining moment. And I fear that with Pau Pau's passing that portal has shut.

As I write this, I text my mom: "I have a question—when people in Cheung Chau would say to Pau Pau, 'Ah-Ling ge lui fan lay,' does it mean that Ah-Ling's daughter has returned home?"

She writes back, "Yes, in that context, Cheung Chau is the base, so Ah-Ling's girl has come back."

OMAR EL AKKAD

Flight Paths

1.

2010

The word for invoice is the same in Arabic and Italian: fattura. We learned this, my mother and I, on the outskirts of a cemetery in Naples, as we tried to navigate the final arrangements for the transfer of my father's body. It was a beautiful day, sunny, the sky Riviera-blue, and somewhere in the periphery of my vision, focused on this undertaker in his ill-fitting suit, there was a family mourning their own newly dead. They were of this place. We were not. Helplessly, my mother struggled to make the man from the funeral home understand what she was asking for, until finally, exasperated, she blurted out the word in Arabic, and the man nodded. By chance, our languages overlapped; we were understood. The man disappeared into a nearby office and, a couple of minutes later, returned with the bill of sale. In a few days we would need to show this document to a military inspector at the Cairo airport, when we returned to bury my father in the city of his birth. For the last twenty-eight years of his life, he had been a migrant and now, in death, he would go home.

I come from a long line of malfunctioning hearts. My grandfather died just before my father was born. My father made it to fifty-six before he died suddenly of a heart attack while on a cruise with my mother and her siblings off the coast of Italy. In the days that followed, as we trudged slowly through the bureaucratic mire, trying to give him the burial he wanted, I found myself slipping in and out of communion with all the lives we could have lived, all those small coin-flip moments that make up an unanchored life.

2.

1986

In much of the Arab world, it is customary for a boy to take for his middle name the first name of his father. My middle name is Mohamed. My father's middle name is Ahmed. It goes like this, as far back as there exists an accurate record.

In addition to being my father's name, Mohamed Ahmed is one of the most common combinations of first and middle names in the world, and it just so happens that there's someone on Egypt's terrorism watch list with the same name. We found this out one morning at the Cairo airport as we awaited a flight to Libya.

Having grown sick of being poor, being hassled by the ubiquitous cops and soldiers that prowled Cairo in the years after the president's assassination, my father did what so many Egyptians of his generation did, and tried to find work in another country. An accountant by training, he eventually accepted a job offer in Tripoli. I was four at the time. We packed our bags, we readied to leave.

Not long after we got to the airport, my parents and I were escorted into the secondary screening area, where we waited for hours until finally the men detaining us became certain my father couldn't be the man they were looking for. By then, our flight had already departed. The job offer in Libya was revoked; my father missed his chance to get out, only to be offered, a short while later, employment as a junior accountant in a hotel in Qatar. He knew almost nothing about the tiny peninsular state that juts out the eastern edge of Saudi Arabia, but he accepted, because what mattered was to leave. A short while later my mother and I followed him to a country that, over the next couple of decades, would become perhaps the richest nation on earth, flush with more oil and gas money than it could possibly use.

This is where I ended up spending my formative years—the Arabic accent scrubbed clean off my tongue by years of British and American schooling—instead of Libya. Nothing I have ever done, nothing I've achieved or struggled for or chased after, has had a more significant impact on the trajectory of my life than a random case of mistaken identity at the Cairo airport a few months before my fifth birthday.

3.

1994

It was a long form full of questions, but the only one I remember was about Nazis. It asked whether my parents or I had ever supported the Third Reich between the years of 1939 and 1945, or something to that effect. We had been vacationing in Florida for the summer and we wanted to extend our stay, which meant reapplying for a visa, which meant filling out one of these forms, an interrogatory listing of all the worst ventures in which a person could possibly engage—human trafficking, terrorism, genocide. Dutifully, we checked off *no, no, no,* always on the lookout for trick questions—"Have you ever *not* engaged in terrorism?"—always aware that we were the only party in this interaction for whom things could go wrong.

Westerners don't tend to think this way, but in the part of the world I'm from, we talk about passports in terms of their power—a metric related to the number of countries any particular citizenship allows you to visit without a visa. The Japanese passport is probably the most powerful in the world; its holders can visit more than 190 nations without having to affirm they've never aided the Nazis. My old high school friends Naseem and Rami, who for a while had no formal statehood and were forced to rely on Palestinian Authority travel documentation, held one of the least powerful. Every border became a carnival of indignity.

To navigate the world this way, roughshod on the back of a weak passport, is to become malleable. One must contort oneself into the shape of the admissible. It's a subtle, delicate art. The smallest hints of an accent, the slightest stuttered syllable or twitch of the eye in response to a question about the purpose of a visit might cause things to topple.

For years, when I worked full-time as a journalist, but before I was granted American citizenship, I entered the United States wielding some of the most bizarre explanations any TSA agent had ever heard— on my way to Andrews Air Force Base to hop a flight to the Guantanamo Bay detention camps, or the time I went to war correspondent training in Virginia before heading off to Afghanistan. But the only time I was taken into secondary and interrogated was when I arrived at JFK and told them I was there to see my cousin. It turns out a lot of terrorists claim they're here to visit cousins.

4.

1998

To live in Qatar as an expat—the word we use when a migrant is too well off to be called a migrant—one must secure kafala, a sponsorship of sorts, issued by a local citizen or company. In order to protect the country's oil and gas wealth, the Qatari government makes it almost impossible for any foreigner to secure citizenship. Most people who live in Qatar are foreigners, and so are subject to this kind of precarious existence, the possibility of overnight deportation always present. Everyone knows the deal: you come here, you make some money, but you're a guest, always. There's no being of the place, only passing through it.

One year, after more than a decade of living in this place, it became clear that our time in Qatar was coming to an end. On the last day of August, we boarded a plane to Canada.

I knew nothing about Canada. My first week in Montreal, I got on a bus and tried to jam a twenty-dollar bill through the coin slot, expecting change. I had no idea how the bus system worked; there was no such thing as public transit in Qatar. I was sixteen and the prospect of starting from scratch—of acclimating to the way the air turns to needles in the lungs when it's forty below zero—was unbearable. The world was an onslaught of beginnings.

5.

2001

For a long time, my father couldn't find work in Montreal. His French wasn't good enough, his credentials insufficient. As we burned through our savings, he expanded his job search outward until he got an offer to work as an accountant in a hotel in Wisconsin, a state none of us could point out on a map. But it paid well enough and there was nothing else going, and so he accepted it. There was some paperwork that needed to be completed—a work permit that, his prospective employer assured him, should be fairly straightforward—and all wrapped up by the second week of September at the latest. Then the second week of September arrived.

The work permit process stalled; everyone knew why. Eventually, the hotel had no choice but to stop waiting and hire someone else. We never moved to Wisconsin. I imagine another iteration of my family moving into that strange, ghostly neighbourhood of would-have-beens, alongside the us that lived our lives out in Tripoli and the us that remained in Cairo. All these aborted trajectories, all these vessels that never left shore.

6.

2010

On a Sunday in August, my friend Anna tried to find an Italian translator in Toronto. In order to take my father's body back to his home, we needed to appease the bureaucratic whims of the Egyptian, Canadian, and Italian governments, and this required, among many other pieces of paperwork, a certified translation of my father's Italian death certificate. In Islamic tradition, the dead should be buried within twenty-four hours, but we spent days wrangling all the necessary permissions before we finally travelled back to Cairo, our first flight together since the day we came to Canada twelve years earlier.

In Egypt, any arriving body falls under the purview of the military. We landed around three in the morning and my cousin and I accompanied the coffin to a nearly deserted corner of the airport, where a single administrator sat at a desk, bored and irritable

She checked the paperwork, the documentation from the funeral home in Naples and the translator in Toronto and the Egyptian embassy in Rome. It turns out we had missed a form, without which we were technically engaged in a crime. It was illegal to have transported my father's body this way, and it was too late to do anything about it.

We stood there for what felt like a long time. Finally, my cousin said, "We just want to give him a Muslim burial."

She stamped the forms. She let us through.

At the mosque in El Hussein, they lined up the coffin next to a half-dozen others, all there to receive the same final prayer from the congregation, and some of the men entering the grand hall mentioned what a privilege it was to have died in these last days of Ramadan, the most blessed month. They seemed genuinely jealous.

We prayed, then we took the body to the place where my grandfather and my aunts were buried. Cairo's city of the dead housed the

living, too, and one of its residents pointed us to the El Akkad mauso-
leum as though pointing out a neighbour. We carried the shrouded
body underground, past the bones of ancestors, past the past. Home.

For years, whenever I thought back to that day, I thought of it as my
father's final migration. But it wasn't a migration. It was something far
more merciful: an ending. It is the most lightening thing, to be done
starting over.

*"Flight Paths" by Omar El Akkad was previously published online in the
Paris Review on May 11, 2022.*

HANNAH ZALAA-UUL

The Land Remembers
All of Its Children

The airplane skidded to a halt, and my heart was heavy. Must be antici-pation or nervousness, I told myself. I could see the washed green plains through the window. So unlike anywhere else, it could only belong to our land. Our home. My heart swelled to see its familiarity for the first time in five years.

Since moving, rebuilding, and returning, my definition of home seemed to reside in the coming and going, existing among invisible national lines, somewhere above water and below sky. Approximately.

I disembarked from the plane, I doubted my language capabilities. Hadn't practised in years and nervously answered questions at the air-port gate, hoping that the admin officers couldn't tell that this was a world I hadn't been properly acquainted with.

In the past, dozens of elders had said to me: "Mongolians should speak Mongolian and not this foreign tongue" and "You should be ashamed to speak more fluently in English than your mother language," which was smugly followed by "Are you even Mongolian at this point?" As if language determined my ancestry, unmaking my blood and DNA.

But the harsh comments stuck with me and every so often the words emerged whenever I stuttered, nervously pronounced words with a foreign accent, or struggled to explain something in Mongolian.

On the car ride to our family home with my older sister and her two kids, I made mental notes of everything that was different and that had stayed the same in the years since I've been away. *Hmm, the roads are better, there's camera surveillance for road safety, there are new taller buildings. More restaurants, chain stores, and coffee shops than I remember from my childhood.* A video call suddenly interrupted my internal monologue—it was my parents, two elder sisters, and friends gathered for a rare virtual rendezvous with me. Basking in their infectious joy, I was eager to latch on to the positive signs of progress in the city, and I could tell through the phone that my family and friends were trying to express the same. They mentioned so often how much has changed in the five years since I've been here. It might have been my imagination, but it was as if they were pleading with me through unspoken language: *See, life here is possible. You can be happy here. You can come back.*

I didn't disagree, but I didn't make any notions to agree, either. The conversation in the car with my sister had been no longer than a few minutes, but it was already building: the pressure, guilt, confusion, sadness, relief, caution, and against all odds…joy and maybe a little hope. I knew, realistically, that one trip in the summer would scarcely undo years of identity crisis and yearnings for belonging, but I couldn't help but feel hopeful. I needed new imprints of memory to remind myself that it was not all that bad, in part to brush over painful memories of feeling like a stranger in my adolescent years, split between Canada, India, and Mongolia. Already numbing myself to all that I was feeling, I tried to relax and clear my head. Eventually, the roads came to pass familiar streets, old libraries I frequented, cinemas with chipped paint, and the school I graduated from. Corridors and halls I fantasized about leaving behind.

The first week passed in a jet-lagged blur as I adjusted to the new-old faces of relatives and friends I hadn't seen since I was a shy, lanky teenager. The awkward pauses that came after the small talk had died down, then the belly-laughing as if no time had passed. My parents' house in Ulaanbaatar, vacant since my brother had moved to Germany for university two years ago, was once again bustling. Mom and Dad were so happy to be surrounded by people and children again. Sisters scattered across the world, one returning from the Philippines, two arriving from Canada, and two of the elder sisters remaining in Mongolia to nurture the legacy of our family.

Our lives had diverged in different directions, driven by educational pursuits, careers, curiosities, love, and for some, the joys of motherhood. Though we were always connected through long-distance phone calls, text messages with photographs and life updates, this summer brought us together in a way that wasn't possible before.

In the years since COVID-19 had begun, it was just my parents in this apartment, a quiet life returning after forty years. They would never tell me as much, but I know they must have felt lonely.

After the tearful reunions, the slight dysfunction and family banter had returned as we got used to each other's company again. Every day was a struggle to find privacy in a house full and busy with my many nieces and nephews. I'd gotten accustomed to napping in odd places at the behest of my mother who wouldn't let me leave her sight since my arrival. I joked to my sister about whether she thought I'd disappear in a puff of smoke if she left me alone. When my sister countered that Mom had missed me, I rolled my eyes in a cheeky, younger-sister way. Of course, I knew. I dealt with complicated emotions the only way I knew how: humour.

I tried to brave an independent journey whenever I could, to do small things to reacquaint myself with the scene. Visited supermarkets and struggled to ask the store clerk, with the limited Mongolian vocabulary in my arsenal, if they have contact lens solution. She was kind enough to explain that the pharmacy might carry one. I still hurl self-criticisms in my head for not being able to communicate well enough and wonder whether she flagged me as an outsider. I couldn't shake the feeling that everybody could tell that I was a stranger; I sure felt like one. I'd stepped too far in the other direction, pursuing a life elsewhere for so long that there was now a palpable distance between my people and me. I felt responsible for it and unsure of how to cross it to get to where everyone else was. Why did every step of building a life in Canada feel like an act of betrayal?

I met with high school friends at their favourite restaurants, listened to their university stories, met their boyfriends, and learned about their exes who broke their hearts and wallets. The girls I knew, already blossoming into independent women. Making their independent path in a country I left behind.

I now recognized the pressure building up to that point as grief. Grief for the person I didn't become. For the stories and milestones I'm not a part of, and for this evolving world I stubbornly didn't recognize. I grieved that this world was moving on without a place for me. If I wasn't anyone here, who was I anywhere else?

Our time together was limited, with every occasion and sightseeing packed into our one-month stay. My parents, my sisters, their kids, and I piled into four separate cars to make our way to Grandma's place in the countryside. The roads outside of the city were narrow with cracks and potholes, forcing us to occasionally veer off to dirt roads while construction workers repaired the pavement. My elder sisters' children had gotten motion sick, and so we tried our best to make the journey as comfortable for them as we could. We stopped frequently for breaks, played hide-and-seek to stretch our limbs, took pictures, and took them on their first camel rides in the singing sand dunes (duut mankhan) on our way to Uvurkhangai province. It occurred to me that the childhood memories I cling to for comfort were happening for them on this very trip. Maybe, in their twenties, they will also think about the dunes, the horses and camels, skipping rocks across the lake, hiking to mountain-tops, and playing with goats—reconnecting with a cherished time when they felt an unwavering sense of belonging.

In Mongolian culture, households present their guests with fresh meat and dairy products as a gesture of respect and hospitality, and in return every arriving guest must have at least a bite. So, in one month, I ate my weight in meat and dairy treats. We connected through food. That's what I love most about our culture, the unspoken ways that we claim each other as our own.

My grandmother's summer dwelling was exactly as I remembered it in girlhood. Her ger—an intricately woven traditional dwelling, at the skirt of Zalaa Uul, the towering mountain with a stone crown at its crest—was my father's namesake. The ger was still situated by the river stream where we used to dare each other to jump across as children, with the same golden dandelions lined around the bank that we used to make flower crowns.

We made a bonfire in celebration of our family reunion, with five sisters together for the first time in thirteen years, on the land that my ancestors roamed with pride, and that my father yearned to return to every summer. Now we yearned to belong and to be found. Every sibling in one corner of the globe. We had learned how to read and write in one place and became adults in another. I had wanted to say how proud I was to be their sister and how much courage I felt in seeing how they embodied all the fragments of their identity unapologetically, with honesty. It made me feel brave to do the same. I often wondered if being so far and different made them feel just as lonely as it made me feel at times. Even now, with all of us situated on different continents, I knew just as well that they too had yearned to meet again in the middle. I doubted if I would be able to say any of these sentiments without crying.

In the bonfire, we whispered our prayers and blessings and asked for strength from the flames. Under the light of the full moon, we prayed for good fortune for our family. I had already started tearing up when my mother shared stories about my grandmother who had recently passed, and broke down into sobs when she embraced me. My father joined, enveloping the two of us, and we cried out all that we kept in our hearts.

In all that time we spent sightseeing, none of us said the words: "I missed you. It was hard without you." And I too had wanted to say, "Look, look what I became, on my own! I did it! It was impossible and I did it!" Which coincided with the even smaller neglected voice of mine saying, "I'm still small and young, and I still need you, doing life without you is not easy." Being with my family under the night sky, on our ancestral land, I knew I belonged.

Here it didn't matter that I harboured guilt for being away for so long, or that my Mongolian was dusty, or that, when nervous, I spoke with a blended Indian, Canadian, and Singaporean accent. It didn't matter that I felt responsible for the chasm between myself and my family members, as we were never accustomed to sharing exactly how we feel, anyway, especially not with one another. My small doubts seemed even more minuscule in comparison to how our lives were in harmonious bond with the land. In the quiet stillness of Khuisiin Naiman Lake, I could laugh at my silly ideas of belonging and identity. The fears I harboured in truly embodying my hyphenated identity didn't have to be a choice between one and the other when so much of me was influenced by both. I could be as fluid and momentary as the passing streams in the river. I validate the scattered, unfinished, cut, and edited parts of me that are equal to this strange abstract whole.

The land is a timeless mother, gracious in her patience and yearning for her children to return. Despite the passing years, how far I might have gone, and how much I've changed, the land will always remember me when I come home.

TASLIM JAFFER

Four Degrees, Twenty Minutes South

For many children of immigrants, "back home" exists in stories, and, if we're lucky to have them, photographs, like the ones Dad dropped off at my house a couple years after Mom died.

My mom's albums of Mombasa, Kenya, are my greatest treasures; I would run back into a burning building for the images of her as a cherub-like toddler, as a college student with ice-blue makeup painted on her eyelids, photos of Nanimaa and her sisters in the courtyard, cooking biryani in huge sufuria, of Maa holding a bandhani pacheri over Dad's head in a pre-wedding ceremony. As an adolescent, I pored over these photos, traced faces with my finger, noted hairstyles, backgrounds, and decor, while Mom brought the moments to life with her stories of back home. I recall her talking about the beaches, and the wind that blew through her hair. Listening to her memories, my brain registered her wistfulness, and the scent of the briny air buried itself in my nostrils. "That wind." Mom would smile, and I would taste it. In Kutchi, you don't say you "feel" the wind, you say you "eat" the wind. When Mom talked about the wind on the Kenyan beaches while the rain pelted the windows of our B.C. home, I'd imagine her gaping mouth ingesting the gusts off the ocean.

With Mom gone, the albums are an umbilical cord to my birthplace and my extended family, feeding my need for a connection to where, and who, I'm from. Beyond the albums, my parents had brought "back home" to B.C. in other ways, too: African art, Indo-African cuisine, and our native Indian language, Kutchi, which, after over a century of being spoken in Kenya, included many Kiswahili words. Even though I was an infant when we left Mombasa in 1979, my first language still sounds like Mombasa, my mishkaki, masala potatoes, and mahamri barazi taste like Mombasa, my oodh perfumes smell like Mombasa.

Though Mombasa has lived inside of me for decades, I've never felt certain that *I* exist anywhere in it, whether my osmotic nostalgia is strong enough, or authentic enough, for me to slip back into my birthplace and be a part of it.

At the beginning of 2019, I was rummaging through a box of my mom's albums, looking for images for a family history project, when I came across an 8.5 x 11 page, folded in thirds. It was a printout of an email addressed to Dad, dated August 2005, from his best friend now living in Diani Beach, across the harbour from their hometown Mombasa. Uncle wrote about how sorry he was to miss their graduating class's upcoming reunion in Calgary and urged Dad to come back home. "Bring your children," he wrote. "So they can see for themselves…the places where we spent our simple but very happy childhood days."

It wasn't the first time I'd come across the letter, but the timing of finding it that day felt significant; I'd been talking to Dad for months about going to Mombasa together. Dad was always noncommittal whenever I brought up a return, unconvinced that seeing his old home was a good idea, despite his fond memories. Friends and relatives who had gone back for visits reported everything had changed. Mom would shake her head and cluck her tongue, the telltale sign of her disappointment, whenever she'd hear this. My parents never went back.

But now, holding Uncle's letter in my hand, with albums splayed around me on my basement floor, I recognized how quickly I'd gotten to this point in my life—forty years old, married with three kids, without once visiting my birthplace—and how quickly and unpredictably the rest of it could go. Mom had already been gone for ten years and I was hyperaware of Dad's age. I called Dad later that day, with renewed determination. "I need you to show me Mombasa," I told him on the phone. "I've never even seen where I was born." There must have been something in my voice that day; he relented and we booked flights departing eight weeks later.

When Dad's cousin learned we were coming, she offered us her untenanted flat, noting that it was newly renovated, air-conditioned, and would be stocked with bottles of filtered water for our stay. I was embarrassed by my relief at these offerings, this subtle acknowledgement of our foreignness. But I wasn't going to give up air conditioning. We gratefully accepted.

The air was warm and humid when my cousin and a driver picked us up from Moi International Airport at 2:00 a.m. My hair dampened around the nape of my neck as we walked toward the car, answering my cousin's questions about the three flights that brought us there. On the drive, I tried to take in what I could, peering out the window, but was met with only darkness. Security guards let us in to Makupa Flats, a gated community built around an Ismaili jamatkhana, but I'd have to wait till daylight to truly set eyes on the place my mom grew up, where my paternal great-grandmother had lived, and where my first cousin still calls home.

After selecting the bedroom off the living room, and sliding into pajamas, I pulled back the mosquito netting surrounding my bed. I relished being horizontal for the first time in almost two days, but a few hours later, I was still awake to hear the morning azaan, a man's voice trumpeting through the dawn air, calling the pious to prayer. I felt my dry eyes sting as the first tears pricked them; I'd never heard the azaan in public at home.

I might have dozed off because my next memory is hearing Dad opening and closing kitchen cupboards and the *tick-tick-tick* of the gas stove. I joined him in the kitchen despite being bone-weary. We fuelled ourselves with strong Kenyan chai and Huseini Bakery nankhatai, then sank onto the living room couch to make a list of landmarks we intended to visit: family homes, places of worship and schools, mostly. Dad mentioned Four Twenty South cottages in Diani, where he and Mom honeymooned—the setting of my favourite photos. "Maybe Uncle can take us there if they are still around," he said. "I don't know if I can find it on my own."

A few days into our stay, our driver took us aboard the Likoni Ferry that inched across the harbour to Diani. Cars and foot passengers were packed together on the same deck, which made it impossible for me to see much from my window except bodies and steel. The drive from Likoni to Diani was a colourful, moving scene of bright fabrics hung on clotheslines, market stalls set up with wares, children running barefoot in the dirt. Snapshot after snapshot of an everyday life that I could only look at through the lens of a foreigner, a tourist with a camera.

Uncle's home in Diani is palatial and set back on a cliff above the beach. The cool tile floors were a relief for my swollen feet. Before lunch, Dad, Uncle, Aunty, and I dropped down the concrete stairs behind their home and walked farther south where the rocky beach meets white sand. We spread out our towels far from the reaching fingers of the Indian Ocean and deposited our hats and sunglasses on them. All that was left to do was give in to the pull of the water; we walked toward the blue-green, the sand like granules of sugar between our toes. I was eager to swim, not just to cool down; until now on this trip, I had only gazed at the ocean from the veranda of Mombasa Hospital when Dad and I went to see the maternity ward where I was born. There I had envisioned Mom's labour, her eyes squeezed tight as she bore down to bring me into the world and give me a first-class view of it upon my arrival.

The Indian Ocean was 28.9 degrees Celsius. It was an invitation, unlike the Pacific twenty minutes from my home, whose frigid waters, even in summer, cause me to tiptoe with dread. Along the shoreline, locals sold hand-carved keychains, hair-braiding, and glass-bottom boat tours. Looking back at the shore from the water, I thought about how a few days before, on the north coast's Bamburi Beach, a local man had approached us with dark objects in his hand. "Jambo!" he called. I returned the greeting. He held up keychains, souvenirs he insisted we buy to take back home. Dad had protested in Kiswahili, brushing him off as politely as he could by saying that we didn't need souvenirs, that we were from there. After a minute or so of this back-and-forth, Dad inched away, turning his back to end the exchange. The man, still talking, followed. I caught the word "mzungu" aimed at Dad who is not a white man, and who, when asked where he's from, has always answered "Kenya." He stopped. I giggled. The vendor turned his gaze to me. From his swift, melodic river of Kiswahili, I pulled the word "ulaya." He laughed when I said nothing in reply. Later, I asked Dad what ulaya meant. "Europe," he said. "He thinks you were raised in boarding school in London." I treaded water, watching from a distance as Dad morphed into a child, splashing water and laughing, with his head tilted back, at whatever Uncle was saying. At a break in their laughter, I heard Dad ask Uncle where the Four Twenty South cottages were. I looked at Uncle, curious. In all our floating, we had drifted farther south, maybe a kilometre from his home. "Oh yeah, yeah," Uncle said, squinting at the distant shoreline, shielding his eyes as he scanned the beach. He pointed. "We're right in front of them."

"What?" I asked. Dad said nothing, pulled a few breaststrokes to shallower waters, then stood on the sandy bottom, rising to his full height. I followed. The waves lapped at the backs of our legs, nudging us toward the shore. Palm fronds beckoned from the grassy slope just past the sand, where sat a stark-white wooden bench with the words FOUR TWENTY SOUTH GUESTS ONLY. When this property was purchased by a British family in 1966, there was nothing but some cottages and coral rag forest, and locating it was easiest by its coordinates: four degrees, twenty minutes south of the equator. Renamed, it became a popular vacation spot for folks like my parents, who honeymooned there in 1977. A couple years later, they cradled me in their arms and boarded the plane that carried us to our new home on the west coast of Canada, fourteen thousand kilometres away. But they never stopped talking about where we came from.

We walked as close as possible to the property without trespassing. I recognized the colonial-style cottages and the gardens. I'd only ever seen them in sepia-toned photographs and here they were, a glorious green. Later that evening, swatting mosquitoes in Uncle and Aunty's backyard, Dad and I theorized about how we ended up there without meaning to. Coincidence? Mom guiding us down the beach, bringing us to where she once stood at the edge of her new life?

On the same beach as Four Twenty South, over one hundred nests are laid by green sea turtles every year. Each nest can have up to one hundred eggs that require an incubation period of fifty to eighty days. A few days after hatching, the baby sea turtles begin an instinctual and perilous crawl toward the ocean. Of the thousands that hatch and set forth on this journey, dodging natural and man-made predators, many will not survive. During their slow migration to the waters, the turtles' brains are imprinted with all the chemical cues around them. This information—the sand, the climate, the ocean currents—is recorded in their brains. Tests performed in captivity have shown that turtles can detect their X-Y coordinates via an internal compass. The female turtles who make it to safe waters travel for thousands of kilometres over the next decade before returning to lay eggs on their natal shores. Sometimes when the females return, they miss the exact spot because the earth's magnetic field shifts slightly each year. That's when they rely on those imprinted cues to bring them closer to where they are meant to be. Turtles go back to their birth shores to lay eggs because their mothers have passed on immunity to their offspring; the babies are better able to resist the parasites of that particular place.

Mom did not pass on any such immunity to me. The night I got sick in Mombasa was when I ate homemade ondhvo shared around a group of women sitting on the benches outside the jamatkhana. Not a fan of ondhvo, but feeling grateful to be part of this impromptu gathering, I scanned for the smallest piece, then regretted it within minutes at the first rumble of my stomach. I excused myself from these ladies, whom I'd only just met, who had welcomed me into their circle with their recollections of Nanimaa's unrivalled sewing skills, and walked the sixty-three steps to the flat in increasing discomfort. As I stumbled toward the bathroom, doubled over with cramps, my body said that, at least in this way, I was not from there. I have the imprints of another shoreline.

NHUNG N. TRAN-DAVIES

The Journey Home

A reporter recently asked my mom if she would do it all over again. Risk our lives by taking all her children to sea in a rickety fishing boat. Come to Canada from Vietnam as "boat people" refugees. I hesitated to translate Mom's answer.

The diplomatic, romantic, heroic answer would have been "Yes." Yes, she would have gone through all the pain and suffering again and again to bring her children to this land of hope and opportunities. After all, my siblings and I have created beautiful lives for ourselves in this amazing country, with all the privileges of warm homes, adequate food, enduring safety, good education, and many career opportunities. I, the youngest of her six children, had become a medical doctor. All from our humble beginnings as boat people, forty years ago.

But her instinctive response was "No." No, she would not do it all over again.

Images of times gone by flashed before me. Images of Mom strangling herself, tightening a belt around her neck, as we young kids frantically screamed and cried for her to stop.

Her answer was heavy, weighed down in part by my own shame. Seeing her aged frame seated across from me, frailer and more bent by the years, her silver strands pulled back in a bun, I understood. It was not easy for a single mother to raise six children in a new, often bitterly cold, land. In fact, it was hard. Very, very hard.

In 2000, I was twenty-six, halfway through my medical school training and eager to travel. What better way to start travelling, I thought, than to do a medical elective in Vietnam? Mom thought so, too, as it was an opportunity for her to tag along. I was only four years old when our family escaped from the ravages of the Vietnam War; it was time to go back to my birthplace, the small city of Cà Mau on the southern tip of the country.

You could say my feelings were a potpourri of angst and joy, dread and excitement. Not only was the political climate of communist Vietnam rather uncertain at that time, but my relationship with Mom was precarious too—complicated by years of turmoil in our single-parent immigrant home marked by the occasional fist driven into the wall by my older brother, lashing out against my mother's strictness. She guided us kids with harsh measures for fear that any wandering on our part would bring dishonour to the sponsors who brought our family to Canada.

The country had just reopened its doors to the West, and we the diaspora were trickling back to revisit the families and life we'd left behind. My heart danced in my chest when our plane touched down, but my mind remained in disbelief. It was surreal for me to set foot on the soils of a land that only, up until then, existed in Mom's stories, news reports, or my own nebulous childhood memories.

I was no longer sure that I could survive a month in this country—a country still pulling itself out from the destruction of war. My very survival depended on my ability to position myself on the toilet so as not to fall into the bottomless pit, all the while pinching my nose and holding my breath to prevent asphyxiation from the malodorous ambience. Alas, you were doubly doomed if you forgot to bring your own toilet paper!

Mom, though, was unfazed. This was her home. I became acutely aware of how accustomed she was to living for years under these conditions, without adequate food or electricity, raising six children, practically on her own, under the constant threats of bullets and bombs. Having hot water, or consistent running water, for that matter, to shower or bathe in were privileges I had growing up in Canada.

Word of Mom's return to Cà Mau spread quickly. And a steady stream of old friends and distant relatives came, some literally from the jungle, to visit mom at Aunty's tube house. Tears poured as we marvelled, embraced, and reconnected after twenty-two years. I learned of a local saying: "Do not pick fights with anyone in Cà Mau, since anyone could be a relative."

Those who remembered me were in awe of how big I was. My cousins weren't shy to laugh at me stuttering and stumbling my accented way through broken Vietnamese. People on the streets knew by my paler skin, my mannerisms, that I was an outsider.

Người Việt Kiều is the word. People stopped and stared and whispered to one another. It was a novelty for them to see these overseas Vietnamese. Little did they know that it was also a novelty for me, seeing a sea of black-haired people who, at a glance, looked pretty much like me.

Their thinner, smaller frames, sun-scorched skin, dusty outfits, worn-out slippers, told the story of the life we left behind. Men and women, stooped by the heavy loads on their back and shoulders, meandering down the dirt roads. Malnourished street kids in tattered clothes swarming with palms outstretched, begging. Not long ago, people here were being robbed and killed for a bag of rice. This was the reason Mom rummaged through our garbage at home in Edmonton, much to our dismay, to make sure that every last grain of rice was eaten.

At the dinner table with my aunts and uncles, I saw Mom in a light that was a rarity in my younger memory—Mom laughing and giggling over shared stories. This was a talkative side of Mom I never knew.

My youth was coloured by the times Mom poured her heart out in despair, as we kids chased her down the snow-blown streets, profusely apologizing and begging for her to come home. The lessons learned from our defiant words or acts of rebellion were harsh. So harsh at times, I buried it. Buried it all, so as to go on.

It became clear that my cousins, who were ten years my senior, knew Mom very well; perhaps, even more so than I.

I had little recollection of my cousins, being that I was so young when we left. I had only known their faces through a handful of black-and-white photographs sent from overseas. They, however, had banked a lot of memories.

These memories came alive on the streets of Cà Mau while I rode seated behind my cousins on their mopeds. As we toured the city, the passing vignettes prompted my relatives to share stories of times when Mom rowed all day to market through the tangles of the Mekong Delta only to discover all of her produce spoiled and rotten from the scorching heat and sun. How devastating that was for her, as she had children to feed. There were stories of how she was blindfolded and dragged by soldiers for the sake of taunting their citizens. And more stories of still harder times that followed after Mom stole away with her children from an abusive husband.

The air was not as hot and humid at dusk, yet it somehow became harder to breathe by the end of these rides, as my heart grew heavy.

The curtain was being drawn back in Cà Mau. I never knew my own father. All I knew was that he died before I was born, and I didn't care to know more. Mom was all I knew and needed to know. I was finally seeing this woman for who she really was. This woman who, back in Canada, toiled all day, all night making meals, washing dishes, sweeping floors, sewing clothes, doing laundry, and so much more.

How could I stay bitter for those times she tracked us down at parties to drag us home to finish our studies while we protested indignantly?

"People can take everything away from you, but they can't take away your education," she would say.

During one of my clinic days at the Cà Mau hospital, a young patient came in for what I understood to be a tonsillectomy. To my horror, the surgeon proceeded to excise and extract the patient's tonsils while the patient was still awake and seated upright. The poor patient gagged and choked, and spat up blood through it all.

Obviously, much in Vietnam hadn't changed significantly in the decades since we left.

I would have to say the same of our struggles as Vietnamese refugees and immigrants to Canada. For twenty years, we struggled to come to terms with the trauma of war, destruction, abuse, and poverty that Mom, and especially my older siblings, lived through. Twenty years on, the scars still haunted us. They infused themselves into every decision, argument, and emotional breakdown.

Now I know that those ongoing struggles were largely because I neither knew nor really understood Mom.

The curtains were now drawn, and through the window, I was seeing a very different woman. I appreciated why she worked three jobs to support us. I recognized the afflictions that made her the person she was, in all her strict and seemingly harsh ways with us. I understood why, at times, she wanted to run away, and even to hurt herself.

It was not easy for Mom to raise six children alone in a new country, with all the challenges of living with low income, a new language, and a very different culture and value system. It was extremely hard—on all of us. But, we survived, then thrived—because of Mom.

A thirty-seven-year age gap separates me and her. We saw and experienced the world differently. She lived through the French occupation, then the Japanese, and lastly, the Vietnam War. I grew up with the privileges of peace, freedom, and opportunities in Canada. I had gone back to Vietnam for the purpose of travelling and doing a medical elective.

Little did I know that the journey would narrow the divide between Mom and me. Seeing her aged frame seated across from me, frailer and more bent by the years, her silver strands pulled back in a bun, I understood. I understood and respected why she would not choose to do it all over again.

I can recall, though, on the return flight when our plane touched down in Edmonton, that Mom smiled. I sensed it was with gratitude. We were home.

MARIAM IBRAHIM

Bullets, Soldiers, and Checkpoints
A Family Vacation

It's a brutally hot July day at the Allenby border crossing, one of the hottest on record, and I'm waiting among the throngs of other travellers, some with wet towels placed on their heads to alleviate the heat, to get into a taxi to take me to my mother's village in the West Bank. The journey from my aunt's home in Amman had taken us several hours, and the time standing in line at the border, waiting as Israeli soldiers use their broken Arabic to order us to go here, wait there, show them our passports, conjures a rush of memories.

I settle into a taxi with my mom and fifteen-year-old niece, not much younger than I was the last time I'd visited, and wait more. Before we can go, our "service," or shared taxi, must fill up with passengers. I've waited twenty years to return to Palestine, yet feel like I can't put it off for another second, especially in this unbearable heat, so finally I offer to pay the driver for the empty seats.

It's impossible to miss the difference two decades makes. The settlements have exploded in number, at times so common I wonder if our driver had taken a detour through Israel, despite having a green licence plate designed to quickly identify Palestinians and keep them out. But no, this is Palestine, regardless of the settler-only buses passing by.

I keep my eyes fixed firmly out the window, determined to take in everything I'd missed over the years. Billboards advertising these illegal communities beckon new settlers. In the distance, construction cranes signal unabated expansion. Usurpers continue their illegal efforts to squeeze out the natives. Two systems of life, separate and unequal.

I also notice fewer Israeli soldiers in Jeeps and tanks on the streets because the last time I visited, the summer right after high school, in 2003, was near the end of the second Intifada. I remember attending protests and funeral marches, getting held up at checkpoints, seeing Israelis detain boys as young as ten, and hearing so many tragic stories of young Palestinians killed by occupation soldiers. Back then, arbitrary road closures and blockades forced us to take wild detours through groves and over hills to reach Nablus and Tulkarem, cities that were each about forty kilometres away from our village. Twenty years later, I don't see as many permanent checkpoints, but the occupation is far from invisible: I see Israeli soldiers standing roadside at various points, dressed in thick military vests and helmets, machine guns at the ready.

As we get closer to my mom's village, memories of many family summer holidays to the homeland come flooding back.

Though they seemed completely normal to me, I've come to realize they weren't your typical family vacations. No hotel stays and tour groups to take in the sights of the Holy Land. No sunbathing at the beach and visits to museums and galleries. With so many relatives in the West Bank—dozens upon dozens of us on both sides of my family— summer vacations, to me, meant day after day of visiting. It meant connecting over meals of makloubeh and molokhia and staying up late, waiting for the heat to break, so we could comfortably enjoy mint tea and platters of watermelon, grapes, and plums. As a family, we'd spend the better part of our entire summers there, and still by the end feel like we hadn't had enough. I suppose that's why I always felt like visiting Palestine was a commitment, and in the past two decades I hadn't found a way to commit. In reality, I didn't need anything more than a plane ticket and a determination that I could—should—go back, even if just for a few weeks.

In my twenty years of absence, I often thought about returning with my mother, who, undeterred by the military occupation, the indignities at the border, the invasive and accusatory questions asked by the officers, still made the pilgrimage nearly every year. So, last summer, when she called to say that she was planning a relatively short trip to Jordan and Palestine with my niece, I realized there would never be a perfect time to go, that in fact now was as good a time as any.

My mother is from the village of Jayyous, just six kilometres from the Green Line, and my father from Qalqilya, a city surrounded by Israel's separation wall. My father was working in a factory in Germany in 1969, when one of the companies that gave Hamilton, Ontario, its "Steeltown" moniker, lured him across the Atlantic. He returned to the West Bank to marry my mother, and they both immigrated to Canada within days. Mom and Dad became citizens within a year.

They were among the first Arab families to settle in Hamilton, where my three sisters and I were born, and where everyone, save for the third child (me), still lives. It's also where we buried my father in 2006.

I don't remember the first time I visited the West Bank. Our summer trips began when I was a toddler and continued through my adolescence. Our journey would usually begin in Jordan. After a few weeks visiting relatives in Amman, we'd embark on an exhausting taxi ride to the border, enduring long queues, first declaring our luggage, then waiting in a security line before finally reaching the front, whereupon Israeli soldiers would search, question, and finally allow us to pass—but not without first reminding us that we were foreigners in our own land. Even as a child, it enraged me, but I knew better than to tell off the cocky eighteen-year-olds holding the indiscriminate power to grant or deny us access to our loved ones.

Travel to and within Palestine was always an exercise in humiliation. Getting there meant being dehumanized by racist interrogations, strip searches, delays for no other purpose than to prove that they held all the power and you held exactly none. Because my sisters and I most often travelled to Palestine with our mother, our first stop was always Jayyous. Making our way there, I'd stare out the window, taking in the landscape and occasionally asking my mother about the strange towns that seemed to have popped up out of nowhere. With their characteristic red roofs, swimming pools, and suburban architecture, the illegal Israeli settlements stuck out like an organic café in a poor neighbourhood. I had travelled these roads so often as a child that I could practically map them out in my mind's eye.

As a teen, I never quite knew how to describe my trips "back home" to my non-Arab friends. Most Arabs knew that dealing with border guards and military was a fact of life under occupation, that at any moment a gun could be pointed at you, that your mobility could be thwarted by an indiscriminate checkpoint soldier—facts so commonly understood that they didn't warrant discussion. Not so for the Jennifers and Ashleys and Emilys. Speaking to them about Palestine required a political consciousness and vocabulary few middle-schoolers possess. Because many of our trips happened during the first and second Intifadas, I was contending with the images of Palestinians portrayed as violent terrorists baked into their minds by mainstream Western media.

"I heard that place is dangerous."

"Isn't there a war going on there?"

"Did you pack a bulletproof vest?"

It turned my summer vacation stories into something much more complicated and exhausting. Once, when I was about eight, I got home from school to find a reporter from the local newspaper in our living room. My mother had brought a tray of mint tea and cookies to the coffee table before recounting the violence we'd endured that summer toward the end of the first Intifada, a particularly traumatic season in Jayyous.

On more than one occasion, our village was the target of Israeli military raids, events that would send fear and adrenaline through my body. As I sat outside one afternoon, overlooking the road leading up to the village entrance, we heard young boys shouting that soldiers were on their way. Some gathered rocks to throw at the military vehicles, and others ran inside as their mothers yelled at them to stay out of the fray. My older sister and I climbed the stairs to the flat roof of our Uncle Salah's home for a better view of the events as they unfolded, spotting a military Jeep pulled over at the side of the road down the hill, an olive grove between us and the intruders. I couldn't tell you how long we were up there watching, but it must have been only a few minutes before the first bullet aimed at my sister arrived, mercifully missing her head and instead piercing the water tank behind us. Everything hung suspended, as if time stopped. Suddenly realizing that more bullets could be on their way, I ran down the stairs, barricading myself in my uncle's bedroom, the only one in the house that locked. I must have been screaming because soon my mother arrived at the other side of the door to make sure I hadn't been injured. I had wanted to be consoled, but there wasn't time for that. As I sobbed, my mother, incensed, told me to remember this feeling. "Tell everyone this is what happens to us in Palestine."

In Palestine, every moment is a lesson, every traumatic experience a crucial opportunity to make outsiders understand just how dire the situation is. And so, when we returned to Canada that summer, my mother got in touch with someone she knew at the newspaper and pitched the story about the local family whose summer trip "back home" was marred by violence. The next day we were on the front page—my mother, father, sisters, and I sitting on our living room couch, my youngest sister, three years old at the time, in front of us with her out-stretched palms holding the spent bullet shells that she'd taken to use as whistles the way our cousins taught us.

And yet, we always returned to Palestine in the summers, despite the dangers, despite the hassles and the indignities and the traumas. As I grew older, I found my anger growing as well, and I felt compelled to do something, anything, to bring evidence back of the treatment I wit-nessed. In one misguided effort at documenting the abuse, I frantically snapped pictures through the window of my Uncle Khaled's home as an invading soldier detained young stone-throwing boys from the streets outside. I thought I was discreet, but soon the soldiers pounded their way into the house, rifles pointed at all of us as they yelled in their broken Arabic to "bring out the camera." I handed it over. My heart pounded as I watched them pull the film out. Unsatisfied, they ransacked the entire home, overturning drawers, dumping the contents of cupboards on the floor and arresting Khaled, taking him on a twisted joyride before later dumping him on the side of a road; he walked through the night before finding a passing Palestinian to bring him back home the next day. I've never forgotten the guilt of that moment, or my searing resentment at the fact that my efforts to capture evidence of our oppression had led to my entire family being punished and my uncle being hauled away.

My family hasn't forgotten it, either, though they recall it with emo-tions much different than my own.

"Do you still have the photos you took of the soldiers when you were here?" Khaled's wife asks me twenty years later. The memory is recounted with surprising nonchalance and levity. My uncle chuckles as he recalls having to find his way back to the village.

"At least they didn't throw me in jail," he says, smirking. The inci-dent has become family lore; the strong-headed Palestinian girl from Canada who thought a few blurry pictures might make all the differ-ence. In the years since, I've come to realize they wouldn't have mattered at all. Images of Palestinians being brutalized by the Israeli military are plentiful. But it would require the person looking at the image to see our full humanity in order to recognize the treatment as depraved.

There's an old joke that you'll always know you've met a Palestinian because they'll waste no time telling you where they're from. It's our way of asserting ourselves, our identity, our existence in a world that's tried to erase us or paint us as violent terrorists. Being Palestinian means being denied the right to exist fully and freely in the place that you come from. And yet here we are, still existing, still fighting, still rooted to the land.

My two weeks this summer have been some of the most joyous memories from Palestine. At thirty-eight, I now look at my family and see my features in the faces of my uncles and aunts—the same almond-shaped eyes, the same weak chin, the same wide smiles—and wonder what took me so long to return. The generosity, the laughter, the time spent together among my Uncle Saleh's avocado and lemon trees, haggling in the souk and eating kanafeh. The late-night gatherings with tea and extra-strong coffee flowing between the stories and memories. It's as if no time has passed at all. The faces of my family remind me that no distance, no injustice, can uproot me. Despite all the reasons for despair, we find joy in every day.

OMAR REYES

Chicken Soup and Tortillas

I was five years old when I heard the sound of metralletas (submachine guns) near my house.

Thinking back, I'm surprised by how decisively I hid beneath my bed without instruction from my nanny, who had opened the front door to let me in. It was a strategic move because once when I was playing in my bedroom, I overheard my parents tell their friends that mattresses can stop bullets. Something about how the wires and cotton fibres entangle the tiny projectiles' spin.

I lay underneath the bed until the gunshots faded, like the tail end of a parade dissipating into the horizon. El Salvador was in the middle of a civil war between the government army and the guerrilleros. The origins of the conflict endured for forty years until a large-scale confrontation finally broke out. This war lasted for about thirteen years, with reported deaths of approximately 75,000 people, mainly civilians. What I heard that day was a regular occurrence for many, including my nanny, a stern but nurturing woman in her thirties, who reached down with her hand and impatiently asked me if I wanted some juice and bread, as if she'd experienced an annoying setback to her routine.

Many middle-income families had nannies during the eighties. They were usually hired from rural and poorer parts of El Salvador to help with cooking, house cleaning, and child-rearing. My nanny, Alicia, wasn't just an employee of my parents; Alicia was family. We both cried when my parents told her we were moving to Canada one day in April 1985.

When my parents retell any story about our life in El Salvador, Alicia is hardly ever mentioned. When you're a refugee in a new country, escaping civil war, living within the poverty line in subsidized housing, realizing your family once had hired help seems painfully humbling and incongruent. A nanny doesn't fit into the narrative of the struggling and suffering immigrant, so she inevitability gets erased from family lore.

But the thing about trauma is you don't get to choose what you want to remember. So, for me, Alicia wasn't erased; her part was just edited to a minor character who sometimes appears within a jumbled traumatic memory of explosions and violence. Whenever fireworks paint the sky with a kaleidoscope of lights, the reverberation transports me back to feeling helpless and terrified. Escaping wars is a misnomer; you never escape them—you just learn to turn the volume down. Unfortunately, on most days, Alicia's reassuring memory *also* gets dimmed down.

My family first settled in Toronto for five years before making the trek to Edmonton, where I eventually went to Bible college. Intent on becoming a church pastor, I paid for school by working part-time cleaning jobs, while earning volunteer experience as a youth pastor. As recent converts to Pentecostal Christianity, we had embraced a wilder version of faith than the stoic Roman Catholicism familiar to most Salvadorans. My parents beamed with pride at the positive impact I was having in our church through the sermons I preached and activities I organized.

But by the time I got my theology degree, I needed a break from the pressure of working at a church. I could see the disappointment in their faces when I told them I didn't want to be a pastor anymore. I needed time away from all of my familiar surroundings to figure out what I wanted to do with my life. How, they wondered, could I have spent all that time and money on a degree I wasn't going to do anything with?

I moved out to Calgary to live on my own and worked at a bank, hoping to save enough to fly to El Salvador that summer. It wasn't meant to be a vacation but a pilgrimage, the kind you take when you've spent five years of your life in college and graduate with a sense of purpose as blank as the symbolic rolled-up paper you're handed during your graduation ceremony.

The last time I was in El Salvador was during a vacation with my mom and my siblings in 1989. I planned to stay most of the time at my maternal grandparents' home in Santa Tecla, a little two-bedroom, five-hundred-square-foot row house with a black metal gate at the front. When I was a child, I remember my abuelito picking me up on top of the stairs and feeling nervous at the altitude. He was the tallest adult. My abuelita, however, was so short that I surpassed her height before my tenth birthday. Every hug from her was like the first in a long time: "has crecido mi Omarcito," she'd say, holding me tightly. You've grown, my little Omar.

It had been fourteen years since our last hug. I arrived at the El Salvador International Airport feeling relaxed and in no hurry to retrieve my suitcase. My dad had warned of thieves and fraudsters who prey on incoming naive tourists. I was naive but I wasn't a tourist; this was my home.

My cousins pulled up outside the airport with their pickup truck and helped me load my luggage. There were more cousins than seats, so I'd be travelling in the back of the truck. Somehow, seeing my seven-year-old cousin mount up short-circuited my anxiety over a thousand different imagined scenarios of collisions and body dismemberment I could experience on the highway to San Salvador.

Returning as an adult felt much different than it did as a child. There was a solemnity in returning to this land as I recognized the gift of having family remain and welcome me back. My abuelita, without abandon, immediately wrapped her hands around my waist when I entered the house, and just like when I was ten years old, commented on how tall I had gotten. My abuelito, never known to smile, merely smirked as he extended his arms to embrace. He seemed shorter than when I had last visited, and you could see it in his cataracts how time had sapped his vigour. I sensed he and I were both asking ourselves the same sad question: why hadn't I visited sooner?

The next morning, while lying in bed in my room, not yet fully awake, I scribbled a few sentences in my journal as a placeholder of all the raw emotions I was feeling. Then I closed my eyes to rest a little. Before I could fall back asleep, I heard a faint and familiar melody outside the window. As it grew louder I recognized it as the voice of a woman singing, with dignity and confidence, "Tortillas! Tortillas! Tortillas!" I had forgotten what it was like to live in a place where music was ever-present and how it smoothed out the rough edges of living in a country devastated by war. This was how I knew my country to be before the sound of gunshots rewrote my memories.

My abuelita poked her head in to offer me some scrambled eggs and tortillas. "Yes," I said like a child dependent on my elders for nourishment, "I'm ready to eat."

Their daily routine was uninterrupted by my arrival. By the time I dragged my jet-lagged body out of bed, my grandparents had already drunk their coffee, eaten their eggs, and picked up pastries from the bakery. I ate what was left, feeling as if I'd entered this liminal space between adulthood and childhood, man and grandson. An adult but also a grandchild entrusted to their care.

The phone rang and my abuelita answered it. Sensing a familiarity in her voice as she spoke to the person on the other end, I gathered my dishes in the sink to give her some privacy.

"Someone wants to speak to you," she suddenly said.

I placed the dishes into the sink full of water and walked toward her. "Who is it?" I asked, sounding as I felt—destabilized.

She just smiled and held the phone in my direction until I took it from her. To make things stranger, my abuelito got up from the table and stood beside me to listen in. "Omarcito!"

My memory scrambled to recall why that voice was so recognizable. In my life, there are only three people who call me "Omarcito": my mom, my grandma, and my nanny.

"Uh...hi, Alicia...uh...I'm in El Salvador visiting. Where are you?"

I wasn't sure what else to say. She quickly filled the silence by asking me when it would be best for her to visit. "I'll make lunch," she said "I am so happy to hear your voice, Omarcito. This has been a dream of mine."

After I hung up, my abuelito explained that Alicia had kept in contact with my grandparents after we'd moved, checking on their well-being, dropping off groceries, helping with house cleaning—all without the knowledge of my family. Even after all these years, and without any compensation, Alicia had been caring for them—and caring for us. "She always asked about your family and you," my abuelito said. "I would update her about how you and your siblings were becoming Canadians and learning to speak English."

"I didn't know," I said guiltily. "Is she doing well? My mom would be so happy to hear from her."

"Alicia has kept herself busy and her son is older now and helps her out." And then, as if to reassure me, he said, "I know she's going to be so happy to see you."

All along, Alicia had faded from our family's collective consciousness, but she, in return, remained presently attentive to us. Standing in my grandparents' kitchen, I felt the heaviness of our absence. Time and distance was no excuse; if anything, it was a reason to keep that connection alive. I knew I was undeserving of her warm and joyous welcome, the promise to nourish me again. I should be the one rolling out a feast for her, not the other way around.

Alicia showed up with a bag of vegetables in one hand and a dead chicken in the other. I was repulsed by this lifeless, fully feathered poultry dangling from her hand, but, my abuelito later explained, fresh chicken was an extraordinary gesture. As I watched Alicia prepare the chicken soup lunch, I was beginning to feel like Canada had protected me from seeing the whole reality of my homeland, much in the same way that grocery store chicken—neatly cut up in plastic and styrofoam packaging—had obscured the reality of farming poultry.

To my surprise, Alicia had barely changed from my last memory of her. There was not a grey strand in her hair or wrinkle on her face. It was only when she moved, slowly and deliberately, that I saw the mark of her age. And she was shorter than I remembered, but this said more about how much I'd aged after sixteen years.

Sitting around the table and sharing stories, I felt like I was rewriting my own sense of history in real time. Our history is not just marked by war and survival, as I remembered it to be, but generosity, loyalty, and hope. Alicia was a war survivor who selflessly took it upon herself to ensure that vulnerable Salvadorians, like my grandparents, were still cared for, and she held tight to the belief that those who had fled from war would one day return. This meal was an act of gratitude.

In that moment, I saw in Alicia the embodiment of what makes El Salvador special. We are the smallest country in Central America, but we dream big. We love deeply and sacrificially.

My father knew that culture is lost when the language is forgotten, which is why, after we moved to Canada, he taught me to read in Spanish and English concurrently. But there's another language that's just as important—an invisible language of yearning and belonging, composed of memories, pictures, emotions, smells, and the intangibility of connectedness to the soil your ancestors walked on. It's not learned; it's lived through. It's the reclaiming of that which was lost and holding it tight.

Before she left my grandparents' home, Alicia and I shared a long embrace. "I get to say goodbye to you two times," she said, "but this time, I'm saying it with happiness."

Alicia, our almost-forgotten family, had shown me at an early age how compassion can be more protective than walls and mattresses. How it changes worlds and overcomes terror. I'd forgotten the potency of these virtues until then. Knowing that she had lived her life in unwavering service to others—to my beloved abuelita and abuelito—sparked something significant within me. I couldn't put words to it right away, not until the final minutes of my trip, when I was on my way back to Calgary, waiting for takeoff. Writing in my journal, I scribbled two sentences that would guide me for the rest of my life: "I want to serve. I desire for my life to be consumed as a servant of grace."

NADINE ARAKSI

Dede's Dream

"Whoa," says my sister, "this famous person on the money looks like Dad when he was young!" She's doling out drams to pay the visa entry fees at the Zvartnots International Airport in Yerevan, Armenia, while I take inventory of my two teenage children, my tired-but-beaming seventy-nine-year-old mother, and our disorganized belongings. I turn for a quick glance—then lean forward for a closer look at the one-thousand dram note. It's uncanny: Armenian poet and activist Yeghishe Charents looks like a long-lost relative. And perhaps he was, though it would be impossible to know without procuring and then comparing Charents's DNA samples to our own. Separated for millennia by the Ararat mountain range, by myriad conquerors, and by genocide, Western Armenians have been ancestrally and physically disconnected from the land that now comprises modern Armenia.

Our family's story, echoing the resilience of the Armenian spirit, is deeply rooted in the 1915–16 Armenian Genocide, which is widely considered to be the first genocide of the twenty-first century, and the mass exodus that followed. My mother's parents, survivors from Kayseri, Turkey, carried a legacy that profoundly impacted our family. My Sahag dede (grandfather) was orphaned, then "adopted" by a Turkish family, and then "kidnapped" by his sister, all before age ten. Desperate to leave Turkey, he sold all his belongings in the 1930s and gave his life savings to a man promising passports to Armenia, a country quickly carved out of Ottoman territory after the First World War—and then quickly colonized again by the Soviets. In effect, there were no passports to be granted. But my grandfather, an uneducated villager, could not have known better. Gathering his wife—my Arşaguhi yaya (grandmother)—her mother, and their two kids, they headed to Istanbul, where neither the passports nor the man they had paid to procure them ever materialized. Stuck in the former Ottoman capital with no money or place to go, their lives as Bolsahays—Istanbul Armenians—began.

The Armenian-Canadian community I grew up in had little to no ties to this new Armenia. They tended to belong to other diasporas connected to Iran, Syria, Lebanon, Iraq, Ethiopia, and a number of other places our Anatolian Armenian ancestors fled to. Because of this, there are now many ways of being Armenian, apparent in the charming subtle differences of our slang and recipes—or the language a diaspora Armenian pulls from when stuck for a word. My dede and yaya pulled from Turkish, which was often met with judgment for employing the language of our oppressors.

Possibly the most misunderstood ethnic offshoot, the Bolsahays had to navigate a complex identity, integrating Turkish culture for survival while maintaining their Armenian heritage. The number of Armenians who never made it out of the country that tried to exterminate them is unclear—it's estimated that 40 to 80 per cent of the 1.5 million Armenians living under Ottoman rule were killed in the brutal and final days of the Empire—but today, a scant sixty thousand Armenians remain in Turkey. I often wonder what it must have been like for my grandparents to live knowing their government and neighbours could turn against them.

Growing up in Scarborough in the eighties, my parents sent my sister and me to Holy Cross Armenian Day School, where teachers did their best to make us understand Armenian culture, language, and history as more than distant concepts. We had a country, this I knew, but that country, established as a sovereign homeland in 1917, had been shrouded behind the Iron Curtain for the majority of its existence. Only the most privileged diaspora folks could access Soviet Armenia. For everyone else, Armenia was an idea imbued with a sense of duty and reverence—a mandate reinforced by parents, family, Armenian school, and our community: that the preservation of our land, its language, and culture was of the utmost importance to our survival. But try as I might, Armenia, to me, remained a mythical land of ancestral pride that I read about in books from far away.

In 1982, Dede died with an unrealized dream born of displacement and longing—to touch the soil of his homeland. Lying on his deathbed in Scarborough, where he'd lived since 1977, he shared his last wish with his baby—my mother.

It would take nearly four decades before my mom, now a yaya herself, would bring us along to fulfill Dede's dream with a small spade and a Ziploc bag discreetly packed in her suitcase.

As the family storyteller, I hoped our journey to Armenia would provide a bridge from the past to understanding ourselves and our place in the world. With Mom advancing in years, our pilgrimage felt urgent. I wrestled with expectations for my own dream: to connect the dots of our scattered heritage and experience the land that was always a part of us yet so far from our realities in Canada.

Yerevan's crisp night air embraced me like a suffocating auntie as we left the airport to meet George, our driver. Originally from Aleppo, George sought a safer life for his family in Armenia, as did roughly sixteen thousand other Syrian-Armenians, when the Syrian Civil War began in 2011. Compared to the customs officers' unfamiliar Eastern-Armenian dialect and Russian-influenced accents, George's soft-spoken Western

Armenian made it easy to converse. With a "Yalla!" he drove us to the Marriott in Republic Square, promising to return later that week for our tour of historical sites.

The realization of being in the land where our ancestors once walked, loved, and struggled overwhelmed me. Everything felt new yet familiar. It didn't take long for me to understand why a growing number of Western Armenians had been repatriating or spending extended periods visiting this small country of three million. Armenia, young in its independence, symbolized resilience and hope. Since the introduction of dual citizenship in 2007, initiatives like Birthright Armenia and Repat Armenia have inspired diaspora youth and entrepreneurs to invest in nation building. The 2018 Velvet Revolution, a peaceful citizens' movement demanding democratic governance, ignited a new vision of Armenia, appealing to the diaspora's youth to shape its future. The allure grew as Kim Kardashian and other Armenian celebrities flocked to Yerevan to help showcase our modern traditions to the world, and, maybe more importantly, prove to the next generation that rebuilding Armenia wasn't just vital—it was cool. Now, seeing the awe on my son's face, gave me hope that, one day, he might come here again on his own accord.

On our first daylight exploration, my son and I climbed 750 limestone steps to look over this stunning city from atop the Cascade. Halfway up, a hillside speaker blared French-Armenian crooner Charles Aznavour's "Hier Encore." We soon discovered the tunes were coming from a museum dedicated to the recently deceased chansonnier. We twirled with joy, the sun beaming on our jet-lagged faces, our iconic Mount Ararat in the distance, and at that moment, Armenia felt like Disney World for the diaspora. I was living Dede's dream in real time.

I'd never experienced a city where everyone, even the statues, looked like family. Sure, the popular look for women in the capital was more Kardashian than Karine from the Ladies Auxiliary church group, but seeing short-statured, dark-haired, big-nosed people like me all around was a revelation. Who would I have been if I'd grown up here? So many of my teenage struggles came from my desire to assimilate. Torn between the culture of my homeland and my motherland, I constantly rebelled against the latter. Home felt like a museum that preserved old Bolsahay traditions, where I had to be a "lady," speaking only Armenian, serving men first at dinners "out of respect," and preparing for my future as the Armenian bride and mother I was expected to grow up to be. Against the push to be a good, traditional first-born daughter, I felt pulled to "just be like everyone else" until the door burst open and I could breathe—the only way to experience Canada was never to be home. But now, staring at centuries-old Armenian artifacts, I found myself imploring them to reclaim me—their lost daughter who had carelessly discarded parts of her priceless heritage with youthful arrogance.

I could see the effects Armenia was having on Mom, too. Seta had practically reverse-aged overnight, insisting on strutting down Yerevan's streets in search of a talked-about light show while the rest of us were ready to call it a night. I watched in awe, her elderly body moving with the confidence of a woman with incredible history, tossing her scarf elegantly over her shoulder to let you know it, too.

The following day brought new adventures as Shant, George's young colleague, chauffeured us in a spacious vehicle to explore remote sites. Shant played vintage Armenian classics, putting Mom in a lively, relaxed mood as she sang along to the smooth sounds of Adiss Harmandian. On our way to visit UNESCO-protected churches and monasteries, we rolled past grassy hills, dotted with sheep or protruding masses of black obsidian. Hits of beauty were abruptly interrupted by eerie, half-built subdivisions and gas stations abandoned when Russia switched from diesel to petroleum, as though the infrastructure had come down with the Berlin Wall.

Each landmark became more than a tourist stop; they were windows into Dede's enduring spirit. At the eleventh-century Kecharis Monastery, "khatchkars"—iconic masses of stone engraved with crosses—stood as powerful symbols of Dede's resilience. The green mountains of Tsagh-kadzor evoked the land of his family's Turkish village, before they were conned into moving to Istanbul, making me wonder whether he would have preferred this forested ski town over a bustling city. Every stop seemed to thread together our family's past as though revealing hidden messages woven into a rug. Lighting candles in every holy place, I wondered if Mom's prayers differed from her usual requests for God to keep us all safe, healthy, and happy. Was she having private conversations with the souls of those who raised her?

But as the days wore on, a sense of diaspora guilt began to sink in. As I stood by the milky turquoise waters of Lake Sevan, about to snap a photo of Mom with her grandson, and imagining how joyous Dede would be in her place, a shrivelled woman selling pomegranate charms approached me. She claimed to be seventy-five, but looked much older. At first, I was impressed—how did she manage this hill daily?—but Mom, of course, saw it as a harsh reality. "Life here is so hard," she whispered to me.

In moments like this, I felt both the weight of our displacement and the relief—we have been lucky to live in Canada. And even when facing the very best Armenia had to offer, a persistent undercurrent of unease lingered. For every "maybe we should move here" fantasy, imagining how far my Canadian dollars might go, a deeper awareness nagged at me: that in Armenia, any sense of stability is often precariously balanced against the backdrop of regional tensions. Whenever things feel the least bit settled here, neighbouring aggressors like Azerbaijan are known to attack, reopening intergenerational wounds and fears of ethnic cleansing.

The anticipation of fulfilling my mother's lifelong promise increased as we neared the end of our sightseeing days. Meanwhile, my children's differing reactions to the trip reminded me that our roots to our motherlands get weaker with every generation. "I'm not going to another church," said my daughter, bored to see that we'd stopped at yet another holy site. Half-Armenian and a quarter each Norwegian and British, my children's roots seem more tangled, stretching great distances with no clear connection beyond the stories of their parents and grandparents. In my desire to give them a life free of the burdens of our heavy history, I realized I expected them to help me carry the culture forward without ever really showing them the way. My sister, seizing the "cool aunt" role, chose to sit out with her. In contrast, my son walked with reverence for every cathedral, humorously engaging with holy men in dark robes who teased him about his obnoxious designer sneakers. Despite our varied travel styles, I knew we were creating lasting memories, even if it would take years for the significance of these memories to fully emerge.

We stopped for lunch at a lush garden restaurant near the genocide memorial. As we waited for kebabs to arrive, my mother took her grandson's arm, announcing her intention. Gardens have dirt, and time to complete her mission was running out. Soon, they were out of sight, and I later learned that she had asked him to hold the bag open as she kneeled and dug in the spot she'd deemed best, scooping the rich soil into the Ziploc bag. When they rejoined us, Mom's face conveyed a cool self-satisfaction and serenity, as though her dutiful act had immediately lifted a burden from her typically hunched shoulders. My mother shimmered with the triumph of a promise fulfilled. As I watched her, I felt the burden of a displaced generation begin to lift off her.

We paid our bill and piled into George's car to pay respects to our ancestors at Tsitsernakaberd, the genocide memorial. Rain trickled onto a dozen massive slabs of stone, each representing one of Armenians' twelve "lost provinces" in Turkey, which leaned over the famous eternal flame representing the 1.5 million lost, shielding our grief. Speakers played "Der Voghormia," the saddest song in the Armenian liturgy. I wept under my umbrella, grateful that we had managed to forge our own space for collective grief.

On the way back to meet George in the parking lot, some local men greeted us and asked where we were from. Their initial friendliness turned to scrutiny upon learning my children barely spoke Armenian. "You didn't teach them Armenian? Is their father not Armenian? What kind of Armenian are they, then?" Though perhaps well-intentioned, I felt an undercurrent of judgment, as though our authenticity as Armenians was still pending evaluation. How to explain the exhaustion of a North American working mom, my struggles with logistics due to ADHD, and how losing a precious day off with them to the one remaining "Saturday school" felt unmanageable, if not unfair to me?

In a busy Tumanyan Street restaurant, a waiter who had recently moved his wife and children here from Lebanon urged us in the most condescending manner to fulfill our duty to repatriate. I whispered to my kids to nod and say "Ayo" (yes) if asked questions, lest the waiter rail against my failures as a mother who had not taught the mother tongue to her children.

"We're not seen as true Armenians here," I said to my sister with an eye roll. Not Armenian enough in Armenia, not white Canadian enough in Canada, and too Armenian in Turkey. At the end of this experience, I realized who I might have been here: a traditional wife and mother, rarely questioning the status quo, or, more likely, an outcast for challenging norms.

I knew in my heart that my encounters with the men at the memorial and the waiter were both motivated by a noble desire to preserve pure Armenian identity. But it resulted in narrowing the definition of Armenian identity in a way that marginalized those of us with diverging experiences. The 1915–16 genocide divided us in almost as many ways as it united us. I recognized my part in what they call the "White Genocide"— the unintentional dilution of Armenian culture, not by military enemies, but by the diaspora's desire to assimilate.

On our last night, we got fancied up for a ballet set to Aznavour's music. It was everything Mom adores: being seen out with her family, enjoying something sophisticated, and going out in style. These aspirations of a higher-class life were not just born of her humble beginnings, but our ancestors' scarcity and hunger for dignity.

Sitting with Mom in the ornate National Opera and Ballet Theatre, I thought back to driving through dusty villages and one-gas-station towns. Gas and water pipes snaked outside spare concrete homes, belying rush DIY jobs. Seeing schoolgirls in meticulous uniforms, clutching leather satchels, echoed the quiet class burdens of my own childhood. "Ah," I muttered, my scalp tingling with shame-filled memories at the sight of their too-tight braids, "never let them see how much you're struggling." I recognized the unspoken rule—maintain appearances and mask your challenges—but there's also joy to be had in defying the pervasive perception of the lowly Armenians that still exists across parts of the world. From stories told in whispers over thick Turkish coffee, to nights spent dancing, singing, and gathering over food, Armenians have done more than merely endure.

This wasn't just a family vacation—it was a homecoming a century in the making. It represented a longer, harder road, a journey that had taken us from the lands of our forebears to the diverse and open skies of Canada. The small bag in my mother's suitcase carried not just the physical essence of Armenia but also a tangible link to Dede that we could now bring back to his headstone at York Cemetery.

My brief time in Armenia gave me a touchstone to my history while opening my eyes to its fragile newness and multi-layered identity. I found Armenia warm and heartachingly beautiful, and also still a country finding its feet amid near-constant geopolitical threats. I left feeling deeply grateful for the opportunity to walk where Dede could only dream of, but just as grateful to return to Toronto, Canada, with its vibrant mosaic of diverse cultures, languages, and experiences, a reflection of who my family became in exile. Armenia helped me to let go of our lost past, find peace in my complicated identity, and cherish the liberty to blend my Armenian and Bolsahay heritage with freedoms I embrace in Canada.

As our plane departed, I gazed at the rugged vista below, my heart swelling with a complicated mix of longing and liberation. In this duality, I found my truth—not just as an Armenian, but as a Canadian, as a mother, a daughter, and a storyteller. Armenia had given me roots, but Canada had given me wings.

LISHAI PEEL

Mother, Land

The return was sharp and quick. One week of jet lag during which my eighteen-month-old stayed awake each night, and I oscillated between exhaustion and a deep sense of awe as we travelled through the desert. It was my mother's sixtieth birthday. I had returned home to introduce her to her grandson and to celebrate this milestone birthday together. But being with her also meant contending with a hard family history, years of separation, and a deep-seated need to distance myself from my Israeli roots.

Although I was born in Israel, I was raised in my father's country, in the grey dampness of northern England. Growing up, my mother often told me that she hated the cold weather, that she missed the warmth and the cypress trees. She missed the olive and eucalyptus trees. She missed the pomegranate blossoms and the irises. She missed her mother. But most of all, she missed the palm trees. In Yorkshire, there were no palm trees. There was bilberry and Scots pine, sweet chestnut, and oak leaf holly. Dog rose and aspen, sea buckthorn and black poplar, white willow, and English elm. But no palm trees.

After my parents divorced, she moved my brothers and me back to Israel during the beginning of the second intifada. The palm trees dotting the airport runway were like a welcoming committee, always the first point of entry into the country. I spent that first summer riding buses that I prayed would not explode and watching MTV on my grandmother's bed, begging her to switch on the air conditioning while she grumbled about the electricity bill. My mother had stayed behind in England to pack up and sell the house. When she arrived two months later, she did not seem to notice that everything in Israel was in full bloom after the first rains of the season. She never commented on how good it was to be back in her home country. The streets smelled of jasmine and citrus, but she did not seem to care. The palm trees danced in the autumn rains, but she never took the time to look at them, not once.

As the intifada raged on, my mother also began to wage her own war. She was fighting her ex-husband. She was fighting her father. She was fighting strangers in the street. Most of all, she was fighting with me. She fought with me about how I was trying to take her place, trying to take control of the house. She repeated the same lines until they became blunt with repetition. *I am the mother. Not you.* During this time, she had her first episode and wound up in the psych ward. My oldest brother, sixteen at the time, moved back to England, refusing to live with the tumult of our life in Israel any longer. It was up to me to keep the family together. But there was no escape from the tentacled reach of her rage. Soon enough the anger inside her subsided and turned into something else, something more muddled. She became lost, not sure who to fight anymore. And I wished her back, even if only so that she could once again wage a war against me.

At eighteen years old, I was summoned to the Israeli Embassy in Toronto. I walked the stretch of Bloor Street between Bay and Spadina, where the buildings towered over me and made me smaller. Less person, more shadow. The wide concrete street was adorned with high-end retail stores—Holt Renfrew, Gucci, Burberry, Louis Vuitton, Tiffany & Co. The security guards who stood erect by the storefronts, ready to open doors and greet the shoppers, did not bother to look at me. With every step closer to my destination, the nerves spread like blood ivy from my belly to my fingertips. At the embassy, the security guard asked several questions that made me stammer. My Hebrew faltered, and, once again, I felt like an outsider in my own culture. I was escorted to another security check until, finally, I was admitted into a small waiting room full of other sombre-faced people.

I was new to Canada, sponsored by my aunt and uncle. As our lives became more difficult in Israel, my mother had thrown all her energy into relocating us to Canada, where her brother and his family lived. She wanted to give us a fresh start in a new country, unmarred by our messy family history. She wanted my older brother to rejoin the family. But within the first year of living in Canada, she was gone, leaving my brothers and I to contend with our nettled relationship with our aunt and uncle. Our presence in their house made us feel like an inconvenience. We slept on air mattresses in the cold basement and felt keenly how much it troubled them that we were there, in *their* space. Nevertheless, they had been generous enough to take us in and the burden of debt rested heavily on our young shoulders.

After five years of living in Israel, Canada was a strange land with strange people who apologized for everything and waited in an orderly line and did not speak too loudly. The buses ran on time and there was no dog shit on the streets, probably due to the extraordinary number of garbage bins everywhere. I landed a retail job and my colleagues at work instructed me to change my name to "Lee" so that people could pronounce it. Meanwhile, at my aunt and uncle's house, the tension was palpable and I tried my best to avoid them. I was also trying, unsuccessfully, to avoid my military draft.

But there I was again. Technically, back on Israeli soil. If they wanted to put me on a plane back to Israel, they would have the power to do it. A year and a half prior, I had completed my Tzav Rishon—my first induction to the Israeli army, a mandatory first step in a country where men have to serve three years and women must serve two. But then I had moved to Canada and missed my draft date. The state wanted me back, claiming me now as "one of ours." How ironic to always be pursued by the feeling of not belonging to my home country, its culture and language and social customs, only to be ordered by the government to return because, as it turns out, despite my faulty Hebrew, my defective ability to assimilate into Israeli culture, I was more than Israeli enough to serve.

My name was called and I was led into a room with a stern-faced, middle-aged woman with pale skin and a blond bob accentuating her sharp features. I told her I prefer to speak in English, and she proceeded to talk in Hebrew, demanding of me explanations and answers that I could barely find strength enough to articulate in English, let alone in the language I had wrestled with for the last five years. I took out my documents and showed her the court order proving that my brother was in my custody. She was not satisfied. She asked me why I was his legal guardian, not because she was curious, not because she was softening to the girl at the other side of the desk whose voice was beginning to tremble like a leaf. She asked me because *she was the state*, and, unlike my own mother, Israel does not let go of its children so easily. In a voice as cold as steel, she asked me the single most damning question: *Where is your mother?*

It was too much. My voice cracked and I began to cry and once I started, it was impossible to stop. Her face was impassive. Perhaps she thought I was faking it. There are enough Israelis who try to evade military duty. I was just another sob story. She reviewed the paperwork again while I tried to compose myself. She had no grounds to hold me there any longer. A woman is exempted from service if she has a child or a legal dependent. The embassy spat me out into the cold, bright day as I was still choking on tears. I walked back to the subway station, knowing that I was free, but never truly free from the grief of estrangement. My mother and my home country were now lost to me.

It had been over a decade since I left Israel and I finally decided to return. I had a beautiful boy, on the cusp of saying his first words, and it was time to surprise my mother and bring him to meet her. I decided to rent a vehicle and drive through the desert with my mother. I'd only seen the Negev once, fifteen years prior. The vistas unfolded before me like a copper-coloured scarf caught in the wind. I was left breathless by the expansiveness I found in the barren slopes. My child slept and my mother talked, filling the car with her ceaseless chatter, as though she were trying to make up for all the lost years, as though she were constantly telling anyone willing or unwilling to listen, "I am here, I exist, you will hear me." With my son, she was endlessly attentive, trying to win him over with her tenacious persistence. She sang songs with him in the car, and, when he fell asleep, she continued animating the afternoon with her moving hands and moving mind, not resting to take pause in her one-sided conversation. The desert, with its vast stillness, its insistence on a reverence for silence, was also demanding my attention. Although I had tried to only remember my life in Israel in fragments, although I distanced myself, ashamed by the political actions of Israel's government, its violent occupation of Palestinian territory, although I conformed to life in Canada, shedding my past and forgetting how I had once loved the palm trees, just as my mother had once loved them, my mother, this land, it had never left me. I was brimming with it. There was no escaping the person who made me and the country that shaped me. I had tried for so many years to shed my history, my blood. But history has a way of not leaving and blood has a way of not lying.

It is several more years before I return again to Israel. I see the palm trees at the airport and they bring me a wave of relief and warmth, like a mother holding her arms wide in greeting, closing them around you.

This time my son is four years old, and I rent an apartment in south Tel Aviv. In the park, my son sees a group of Israeli kids of Ethiopian descent climbing onto the roof of a maintenance shed. He begs me to help him climb up with them. They reach out to give him a hand and the children stand on the roof, triumphant faces under the glare of the punishing July sun. They speak to him inquisitively, inquiring what his name is. He speaks not a word of Hebrew, but children have a way of making do when they want to play together. Off he goes with the children, his head of golden hair bobbing up and down as he skips and hops his way to the playground. I am amazed by his ease, the way he can freely navigate his surroundings. I, too, feel at ease, despite myself. I speak Hebrew with a fluidity that is surprising considering I haven't spoken it for fifteen years. Perhaps I had missed the language, perhaps it was no longer lodged in fear the way it had been at the embassy all those years ago. I take my family to the beaches in Tel Aviv, I kiss my grandmother, I eat the foods I had missed. There is a familiarity that softens me. This land, occupied as it is, scared as it is, politically charged and full of problems as it is, is still my mother country.

The trip to the desert during the winter a few years prior and the summer stay in Tel Aviv now shifts something inside of me. After driving past walls of towering cacti, through wind-worn rock formations and cracked, scorched land, after walking with my child through a crush of poppy fields, their red bloom bobbing in the gentle wind, after swimming with my child in the cold winter waters of the Red Sea, after getting lashed by the wind in Mitzpe Ramon, after feeding a camel from my open, sweaty palm, after pinching fresh pita between my fingers and scooping dollops of hummus, masabacha, and labene into my mouth—the Arabic foods I had missed the most—after negotiating deals with the shop owners in Jaffa, after riding a pink bicycle along the Tayelet as my shoulders crisp and burn, the Mediterranean shoreline glistening to my left, after eating homemade moufleta with matbucha made by my

Moroccan aunt, while my uncle shows me all the olive trees surrounding his house and complains about how big they grow, after trying on a million pairs of cheap sunglasses in Shuk HaCarmel, after obligingly listening to a dozen taxi drivers complain about the cost of living, after being called a terrorist-sympathizing bitch for voicing concern about continuous Palestinian displacement, after being stung by a huge white jellyfish that lumbered along beside me in the warm waters at Banana Beach, after savouring the taste of fresh, soft cheese with warm olives and pita for breakfast, after plucking an unripe pomegranate right off the tree to show my son, after watching the palm trees lining the airport runway fade from vision until there is an ache of longing inside me, just as my mother had ached for those palm trees all those years ago in England, after all of this, I leave Israel with a deep understanding that my home country has always been a part of my story, just as my mother has always been a central character in my life. I am resolved to no longer hide from where I come from. We all live with our mothers in our bodies, even though we have travelled so far from the day we once belonged to them.

OMAR MOUALLEM

Hooky in
the Homeland

"Are you going to Friday prayer?" asked Amal, my grandparents' care-taker. I looked at Teta and Gido sitting beside me on the balcony while I considered my options. I'd arrived last night and felt it too soon to offend my elders and start rumours about myself, the heathen Cana-dian, so I said sure. "Good," she said, "I'll leave you some hot water so you can make wudu."

I needed to freshen up after a day of travel, anyway, and was eager to explore my family's hometown alone, something I'd never done before. It was my first trip to Lebanon in eight years and my first as an adult. Fresh out of college, I'd planned to spend the previous summer here to figure out what, if anything, I could do with two certificates from two separate colleges and little life experience. I was prepared to extend it a year if time allowed it. But six days before my departure flight, on July 12, 2006, Hezbollah militants instigated a war with Israel, whose govern-ment retaliated with predictable cruelty; in addition to killing scores of civilians and wiping out entire families, the Israeli Defense Forces tar-geted civilian infrastructure, including runways at Beirut's Rafic Hariri

International Airport—which had just been renamed in honour of its prime minister assassinated by an agent of Hezbollah with suspected Syrian backing. So, instead I spent that summer educating myself in Middle Eastern history, psyching myself up for the rescheduled trip a year later, and enrolling in yet another college—my third in three years.

People told me I was crazy or brave to still go, but if not that summer, then when? The situation, I agreed, would likely get worse before it got better—but would it get better while I was still a wandering young adult convinced that my hidden potential lay dormant in the homeland? Well, at least shave your beard, advised an uncle before I left, concerned that I'd be mistaken for a Shiite—i.e., Hezbollah sympathizer—especially in Kab Elias, our predominantly Sunni town with some Christian neighbourhoods in the foothills of Mount Lebanon. I told him *never*; my beard had been my defining feature since the ninth grade. It signified my proud Middle Eastern identity in defiance of anyone who'd, joking or not, call me a terrorist, and, if I'm being honest with myself, in defiance of my own failures to embrace my heritage. Abstaining from alcohol and reading Arabic was hard, but I could still distinguish my Arabness with basic grooming.

The advice continued after landing in Beirut. My uncles and cousins reprimanded me for my beard on the drive from the airport the night before, and I'd heard it again from Amal and my grandparents on the balcony—which upped my motivation to get dressed and get going.

With a slim digital camera and notebook in my satchel, I bid them goodbye. I never intended to go to Jumah; I planned to see the town, revisit childhood memories, and return home after prayer finished.

My first order of duty was to buy cigarettes for a fraction of the cost that they were in Canada. I stood in line behind a kid who couldn't see over the counter, yet could buy a pack of Viceroy for his dad (one hopes). Not recognizing any of the brands myself, I asked for the same when it was my turn. The clerk, who I vaguely remembered as a distant relative named Karoomi, did a double take. "You're Ahmed Mouallem's son," he said, then proceeded to remind me how chubby I was in the seventh grade. "Look at you. You've lost weight." Karoomi dragged his knuckles across my cheeks. "What's this? You look like a terrorist." We laughed about it and caught up for as long as my limited Arabic allowed, and then I was on my way.

I didn't get far before running into Ghassan, another distant cousin, who used to own a billiards and arcade room. Once, when I was seven, walking around his store, my foot slipped out of my flip-flops onto a sharp, rusty dustpan and was sliced open. Ghassan rushed me to the hospital for stitches and a tetanus shot. Fifteen years later, it was the first thing he remembered about me. I offered to show him the scar, but he was busy looking for his cat, so beautiful, she was, that Ghassan was convinced someone had stolen her.

I suggested he print posters of her and offer a finder's reward. Ghassan liked the idea and asked me to help make some posters. He took me into his house to choose a picture from his son's computer. While his son booted the computer up, I scanned the teenager's bedroom walls. Amid posters of Brazilian soccer all-stars, there were pictures of Hezbollah leader Hassan Nasrallah with his fist raised. Three flags sunk down from the ceiling—Lebanon, Brazil, and the yellow Hezbollah emblem with the *A* in Allah rising up into a machine gun. You'd never see these decorations outside of a Shi'a home a year or more ago. Many, if not most, of my relatives in Kab Elias have portraits of Rafic Hariri or his prodigal son, Saad. Nasrallah was a parasite to them. Clearly the 2006 war was changing his public image. Creeped out, I wanted to leave, but first I had to survive a hundred pictures of his kitty, and, each time, had to remark on how beautiful she was. The call to prayer mercifully intervened. Ghassan offered to take me with him to mosque, but I said I needed to run home and make wudu first.

"Hurry," he said, "there's not much time."

On the way out I saw another Nasrallah picture, framed and mantled where most people keep family photos. Ghassan caught me glancing at it, and, smiling almost tenderly, said, "You look like him with your glasses and beard."

I slipped into the procession of worshippers walking through traffic, then slipped out at the last intersection before the mosque. It didn't take long to reach the outskirts of Kab Elias. I wandered through the industrial area toward a strip of undeveloped land and unfinished family apartments representing the unrealized dreams of émigrés like my father, who left Lebanon vowing to return. They bought the land, started building, and either ran out of money or changed their minds. For my father, it was the latter, and his dream project never broke ground. I saw the empty plot on the highway (pointed out to me by my uncle the night before). In my lifetime, its only use was as a parking lot for tanks by the occupying Syrian army, until mass demonstrations following Hariri's assassination pressured President Bashar al-Assad to end the twenty-eight-year-long occupation.

I paused to photograph an Arabic STOP sign, thinking it might earn me some traveller clout if I posted it on Facebook. As I took photos from different angles, a mechanic across the street came toward me, shaking a big wrench. "Ey!"

I looked at him, then behind me, around me, and back to him.

"Ey! Come here!"

I waved at him happily, stupidly, which had the intended effect of chilling him out.

"Where are you from?" he asked.

"Canada."

"Canada?" he asked, instantly friendlier. "What are you doing?"

"Just taking pictures of things for my friends."

"No, here in Kab Elias. What are you doing?"

"Visiting family."

"What bayt are you from?" His eyes lit up when I told him which household. "Bayt Mouallem! Are you Ahmed Mouallem's son?"

Suddenly, he'd forgotten that I was a suspected national security threat. With a vigorous handshake and a hearty "Ahlan wa sahlan," he welcomed me back home.

The whole exchange lasted a minute, but prepared me for the next time I took out my camera not much later. It was a cemetery wall that caught my eye on account of the curious graffiti on it: a bunch of Hotmail addresses spray-painted for reasons I didn't understand but found terrifically hilarious. Unfortunately, though, the hilarity was hard to explain to the barber in the adjacent building. He jumped down his steps, got right in my face, and demanded that I tell him who I was and what I was doing. With my wretched Arabic, I could only describe my fascination with the wall as, "It laughs."

"The wall laughs?" he asked, baffled.

"Yeah, the emails on it. We don't do that in Canada."

"You're not Lebanese."

"No, not Lebanese. Canadian," I said. "From bayt Mouallem. Son of Ahmed Mouallem."

"Mouallem! My son married a Mouallem. In Canada, too. Do you know her?" He mentioned her name, and indeed I knew her very well. We grew up together in northern Alberta. As I connected our family trees, his grin suddenly inverted, as he appeared distracted by a concerning thought. "Why did you say you are not Lebanese?" he asked.

"I'm Lebanese here," I said, pointing to my head. "And I'm Lebanese here," I said, pointing to my heart. Then I pointed to my lips and said, "But here, I'm not so Lebanese."

He laughed. "I can hear that." The barber then advised that I be careful walking around alone with my camera—and beard. Times are tense, he explained. People will think I'm a spy.

I decided my fellow Sunni Muslims were too paranoid and nosy, so I started hiking uphill to the Maronite community, but all along the way, and even once there, I was scrutinized with what felt like more intensity. The eyes of deceased soldiers staring back at me in photos adorning saintly shrines did not calm my nerves. People behind me whispered, "Who's that?" which prompted me to do something completely benign like talk to wild chickens, so that, at the very least, they'd think I was a "simple" terrorist.

The only people who seemed not to give a shit were three soldiers on foot. "Marhaba," I said as we crossed paths. They nodded their heads in unison at the bearded spy and kept walking.

The view of the Bekaa Valley was spectacular. The red tops of the buildings stretched into farmland, then another small town just like it, then the Anti-Lebanon Mountains bordering Syria. From the speakers in the minaret hundreds of metres below, I heard the Friday sermon and prayer wind down. A crowd spilled out of the mosque and now it was time for everyone to return to work or home, myself included.

On my way back, I spied a man watching me from his window. He disappeared, then reappeared in front of me. I offered my declaration of place, family, and father again, but it fell short. So, I told him who my mom was, and as luck would have it, they went to junior high together thirty years ago. I accepted his invitation for coffee, which seemed sincere at the time, but I now think was probably feigned hospitality that I was expected to decline. But I accepted.

Arm in arm, he led me to his apartment, introduced me to his family, then asked his son to gather his brother's family from upstairs. We had a rickety conversation about life in Canada compared to life in Lebanon, translated through his niece Nadine, who was also delegated to dote on me with offerings. Again and again, she disappeared into the kitchen and reappeared with a platter of fresh cherries, plums, Turkish coffee that she placed in front of me, and refilled before it emptied.

Their generosity became satirical after I complained about the costs of cigarettes in Canada, and how happy I was to buy them at a dollar a pack in Lebanon. "But I don't know which brand is best yet," I said.

"Nadine, go get him the cigarettes," her uncle said, embarrassing us both. I assured them that it wasn't necessary, but soon Nadine replaced my fruit tray with a platter of every cigarette brand. He insisted I try each one. I couldn't tell if this was a teachable moment about the harms of smoking, but I went ahead. One by one, I picked a brand, put the cigarette to my lips for the patriarch to light it, smoked a bit, snuffed it out, and let him light another. Overloaded on nicotine and coffee, I felt light-headed and shaky. I realized the only way to escape their hospitality challenge was declaring one brand superior to all others.

He kindly handed me the whole pack of Lucky Strikes. "It's yours."

I thanked them all for their generosity and promised that I'd drop by again.

"But shave, all right?" he said, sincerely.

"I'll think about it."

By the time I was approaching my family's apartment building, I'd been gone for three hours—far longer than Jumah prayers. As I considered my alibi, I spotted my cousin walking on one side of the road and his dad driving slowly on the other. They seemed to be searching for someone. My uncle stopped the car, hopped out, and called for his son. "I see him." Then he turned to me, looking unusually angry. "Get in the car."

As far as I knew, they weren't religious, so I couldn't understand why they cared about me playing hooky with Friday prayer. But I did as I was told. My uncle launched into his tirade. "You're going around taking pictures? What were you thinking? You can't do that. Do you know what the state of Lebanon is like? People are very afraid. They're looking for anything unusual. And you! You walk around with your beard and bag and camera. A yellow shirt?"

I looked down at my shirt, and, yeah, I guess it was yellow.

"You look like you're from Hezbollah!"

"I do?"

"Yes, you do! And what else? I go to the barber and he tells me he met my nephew. My nephew, yes, taking pictures of a wall. Why are you taking pictures of a wall?"

"It laughs."

"The wall laughs? He thought you were a spy. And what else? You weren't at prayer." He continued, "We thought for sure the soldiers saw you and arrested you."

"Actually," I said, trying to hide my amusement, "I did talk to soldiers. Three of them. I said marhaba."

"And?" he asked, surprised.

"And here I am."

My comedy of errors was practically folklore that summer in Kab Elias, exaggerated and elongated with every iteration. Due to my stunted Arabic, I was rarely the storyteller. I'd sit silently with a forced grin as people told their versions of it. In each case, I was always yelled at by the barber. Sometimes I was chased by him. In one inexplicable version, I was spotted talking to someone in a red truck, getting in with him, and driving away.

The rumours were reinforced when the barber himself would come over for family dinners. "Hey, it's your friend," Amal joked when he walked in. "Nasrallah!" he'd call me, then turn his handshake into a citizen's arrest by pinning my hands behind my back while everyone laughed. If teasing me was an elaborate scheme to get more clients, it worked. I went in for a shave and was never called a terrorist again. At least not in the homeland.

STEVEN SANDOR

Hungary, 1984

When my parents got to Canada, they arrived in a country that was not yet known to immigrants as a safe haven. It was a country wrestling with the notion of welcoming so many people from another country at one time. The stories from the Hungarian Revolution, the romance of freedom fighters tossing Molotov cocktails at Soviet tanks, had won over the Canadian public, but there was still the issue of what to do when all of these people actually arrived in the autumn of 1956.

My parents married in Austria, inside a small church by the refugee camp they'd been living in for a few weeks. This, they learned, would help ensure that they would be assigned to the same destination in the Western world. Initially, that was the United Kingdom, but refugees at that time were allowed to trade their tickets. So, when my mom learned that her two brothers were going to Canada, my parents traded spots with two people who wanted the British Isles over the long trip to a cold country they all knew very little about.

Once my parents arrived in Canada—a Canada that did not yet think of itself as a multicultural mosaic—they were told that they had a year to learn either English or French. That they had to assimilate and fit in.

And a generation of nearly forty thousand refugees took it to heart. In Canada, names were changed to be more, well, English. A generation of kids were born to hyphenated Hungarian families who tried their damndest not to be too Hungarian. Being sort of Hungarian was okay, but saddling the kids with a ridiculously difficult language that hardly anyone spoke was not worth the price of cultural preservation. They were preoccupied with thoughts of not sticking out or being seen as a burden.

So, I'd always seen my Hungarian-ness as something I could take on and off, like a coat. I went to Hungarian school on Saturday mornings in Toronto's Kensington Market, but the language wasn't all that important to me. It was a chore, like someone being forced to attend church to keep up appearances.

Today, you'll go to Hungary and find many flags with holes cut out of the middle, right where the red Soviet star used to be until 1990. The message is obvious: it's saying "never again" to communism. But, to me, it also symbolizes our defiance in the face of being forced to belong to *anything*. I'd argue that there aren't many additions you could make to the flag without Hungarians bringing the scissors—not even a red tin of sweet paprika.

To be a hyphenated Hungarian means being constantly suspicious of one's own Hungarian-ness.

That's something I've come to realize over the years. But, when I was thirteen years old, going to Hungary meant giving up a summer of baseball and hanging out with friends. It was a place that wasn't as exciting as Disney World or even Niagara Falls.

I made my first visit to Hungary in 1984, at age thirteen, on a big family trip with my mom and dad. Reagan was president and the Cold War dominated my thoughts. Everyone I knew was totally fucked up by *The Day After*, a TV movie that educated the masses in how we'd all burn and cook and fry within minutes of NATO and Soviet forces declaring World War III. And, as the film showed us, if you'd survived the opening salvoes of a nuclear war, well, you'd rather be dead.

So, it was weird to be behind the Iron Curtain, thinking that across the ocean "our" missiles were pointed at me. Our family vacation felt a little like pointing a gun at our own heads.

My parents were aghast that I had managed to smuggle a Los Angeles 1984 Olympics T-shirt into our luggage, and told me that I was in no way going to be allowed to wear that thing in public. After all, Hungary was one of the Soviet-Bloc countries boycotting the Games. Advertising those very games, with a shirt with blue and red stars all over it was just asking for trouble.

Growing up in Canada, with so much American cultural influence, we learned that military operations are often top secret; prototype airplanes, the newest tanks and the mobile missile launchers were kept away from the prying eyes of the public. When you crossed into the Bloc, a Soviet-led military force had no use of keeping itself a secret. Some of you are old enough to remember those old new broadcasts of Mayday parades from Red Square. Soldiers marched in columns, followed by tanks, missile launchers, and pretty well any killing machine the Soviets could wheel through Red Square.

In Budapest, one of the big tourist attractions is the Citadel, a monument atop the Buda Hills. From there, you get a panoramic view of the Danube splitting the city in two. But, back in 1984, it was surrounded by soldiers, tents, and camouflage netting—a military exercise in plain sight.

Almost all Hungarians drove cars made in the Bloc: Škodas, Ladas, Romanian Dacias, or Polish versions of Fiats. My grandfather loved his Škoda, a beige-coloured Czechoslovakian death trap. The slightest turn made the car lurch like it was going to roll over. It shook when the key was turned in the ignition. Later in the trip, the axle broke while we were on the road. It were as if Kafka himself had imagined this thing as a joke about the trivial nature of life.

We were all inside of this hellbox, on our way from Budapest to Eger, an ancient city that's one of the great tourist spots of Hungary, a place that defined the battle lines between European kingdoms and the Ottoman Empire. Eger is a city with prayer towers and minarets that has changed hands between empires over the centuries like a third-line hockey player being sent from team to team.

My dad sat next to my grandfather, with my mom and me in the back. I was mad that I didn't get to go in my Uncle Lénard's green Polski Fiat, because he drove the hilly roads like he was auditioning for an F1 seat.

We had to slow down for a roadblock. We were in the middle of the country, with farmers' fields on either side of the two-lane highway. Then, *it* came across the road in front of us. A tank. A real Russian tank. Red star and everything. Rather than tracks, it had big fat tires.

An officer came up to the car and knocked on the window. My grandfather rolled the window down. The officer peered inside the car, and then turned at me, studying the strange Hungarian teenager before him, whose New Wave fashion sense, I'm sure, must have appeared to him like a beacon of my not-from-Hungary-ness. "Excuse us," he said in English, and further to our surprise, without a hint of an accent, "you will have to wait a few minutes, we're having war games."

War games? Right by the highway? I thought, *This totally makes my day.*

But it got better. "How old are you?" asked the officer, looking straight at me in my Duran Duran–inspired headband. "Thirteen," I said.

"Would you like to ride in a tank?"

Before I could say, "YesyesyesHELLYESyesyesyesyes," my father—the voice of reason, the man who repeatedly told me never to trust people in uniforms, including the police officer who came to my elementary school class to teach us not to talk to strangers—coldly intercepted the nice communist's offer: "No, he would *not*." He turned to me from the passenger seat and gave me the sort of look that suggested I might not want to speak for a while.

It never took my dad long to go from the person who killed fun to James Bond.

Except James Bond would never have been caught dead in a place like Lillafüred, the sleepiest of resort towns. Really, it was only a small village, located in the Bükk Mountains in the northern part of the country—a small lake surrounded by lush forest.

My families—that is, both my mother's and father's sides—decided that this would be a good place for a retreat. We all stayed in a series of cabins near the lake.

The evening we arrived, my cousin Eve and I went to the shore hunting for empty Traubisoda bottles. A couple of guests walked by, carrying fishing tackle.

They stopped, looked at my cousin and I, and spoke to me not in Hungarian, but in perfect English, making what my thirteen-year-old brain perceived to be small talk. Just two harmless fishermen asking me how old I was, who I was visiting with, and whether I was enjoying my stay. Then they were on their way.

Later that evening, I told my dad about it. "Funny, Dad, I think there's a couple of Canadian or American guys staying right next to us."

My dad's face turned a particular shade of red. "Come with me, son." He took my hand and walked the grounds until we saw the fishermen walking into their cottage. My dad had a special kind of walk when he was angry, like he was about to begin a sprint, but never quite gets there. Each step was more like a lurch.

He followed the fishermen up the steps to their cabin door.

"Look, I understand the KGB might want to follow my wife and me. But, *do not speak* to my son ever again. Is that clear?"

We didn't see the fishermen again. We were told by the innkeeper they'd checked out that evening.

At least there wasn't World War III.

MAKDA TESHOME

In a Land Far, Far Away

Disney World. That was *the* trip I wanted to take as a little girl. Every year or so, someone from school or daycare would come back from the park, bragging about how they got to meet their favourite Disney character and stay up late to watch the nightly fireworks. One friend had the chance to stay in Cinderella's castle, and, despite not remembering the exact amenities they had, I do remember picturing it to be like a real palace—with a wide, rounded staircase that led to a huge ballroom with sparkling marble floors. Every year, I would tell my parents about these trips that my friends were taking, and every year they placated me by saying that we would go visit the next year. Next year would come and they would promise me the same thing. Finally, when I was twelve, they told my younger brother and me that we would be taking a trip. Back home. To Ethiopia. That summer.

While our parents wanted us to be excited, we already had preconceived anxieties about the trip and meeting a bunch of relatives who knew of us more than we knew of them. Growing up in Scarborough, a diverse district in Toronto, the majority of the kids I went to school with were also children of immigrants and could understand the complex identity of being both from here and over there. So when the summer neared and we spoke about our vacation plans, there was always someone going "back home."

It's an interesting phrase: "back home." Within these two words lies this idea of belonging, of *returning* to a place that is familiar, warm, and safe. To me, the country of my origin was almost like the setting of a fairy tale—a land far, far away. My relatives I spoke to every few months, primarily due to strong coercion, were characters in this fairy tale. From the sound of their voices over the phone and the stories my parents recounted, I'd conjured an image of what they might look like.

I remember landing in Addis Ababa and realizing that I had never been to a place that had so many Black people. However, despite people looking like me or a family member of mine, I still felt displaced by the locals. I kept wondering what about me tipped them off. *Is it the way I walk?* I thought to myself. *Maybe it's the way I dress?* I continued. *But I'm not wearing anything flashy!* Still, people would stop and stare, their faces contorted, while they looked at my brother and me, as if trying to count all the little ways we were not really *from* Ethiopia. Till this day I don't know what they saw.

In Addis we stayed with our elderly aunt and uncle, Sebete Howboy Fita and Howboy Haddish. We rarely went out unless it was to see other family members in their homes. So, when my mom told me I would be going to the marketplace with her, my cousin, and Fita to buy myself a zuria, I was overjoyed. Before arriving at the market, I was continually instructed by all the women to keep my mouth shut; my Canadian accent would give the owner permission to jack up the prices. It was an open-air marketplace that covered maybe two blocks of land, with multiple storefronts on either side of the unpaved walkway. Some carried more traditional zurias—white, thick, long, woven-cotton dresses, the only colour being around the neckline and down the middle of the gown.

Sometimes the store owners would be sitting at the front of their store, with a fabric book in hand, informing shoppers of a sale. My aunt knew just the store to go, and, despite being the youngest of the group, I found it difficult to keep up with her quick, determined strides. When we got there, the shop owner showed us what he had in stock. My aunt went straight for the traditional zuria, holding up one that was dark blue, with long, billowing sleeves, and shapeless besides the scarf tied at the waist. Resigned, I took the dress and went into the mirrorless fitting room—a small space in the back of the store. When I came out, her eyes lit up. "Betam konjo," she repeated as I walked to the mirror. I thought the gown drowned me. Like I had raided my mother's closet.

As my aunt pulled the dress here and there, my eyes were drawn to a mannequin that wore a sleeveless zuria. Like a bikini, it had thick cotton straps to be tied around the neck, and, instead of being mono-chromatic, it was white with light blue embellishments at the waist and ends of the dress. Form-fitting instead of what I thought was frumpy. I plucked it off the mannequin and quickly showed my family before heading straight to the back of the store and vanishing behind the thick blue curtain. Despite the fitting room being small, and having no mir-ror, I knew, even before slipping the material over my head, that I would love it. To my surprise, when I showed my family, they all agreed. As I walked back to the dressing room, I couldn't help but think that the whole process was too easy. Little did I know, a small battle was brewing at the front of the store.

When I met the two armies, the store owner asked in Amharic if I really liked the dress I had just worn. I nodded and whispered, "Ow." Right at that moment, I could tell from my family's reaction I made a mistake. The man had already suspected I was a ferenj (foreign), but now, thanks to my accent, his suspicions were confirmed, and he increased the price. In a stern voice, my aunt told the store owner off before grabbing my hand and leading the rest of us back onto the street.

"The price was too high for a zuria," she told me. We walked all the way back to the main road where my howboy was waiting in his car. Upon seeing us, he stepped out and listened while Fita told him about the whole ordeal. He turned to me and asked if I *really* wanted the zuria. When I nodded yes, he marched straight to the store without us and came back moments later to reveal that the owner agreed to drop the price. It was still more expensive than what a local would get, but not ridiculously so. Over dinner, I learned how my howboy was able to negotiate the price. He had told the store owner he should be ashamed of himself for trying to cheat a young girl out of a dress. Especially one who was visiting her motherland for the first time.

I remember the day we met my mother's eldest brother, Tewodros, who went by the nickname "Teddy." In my fairy-tale imagination, I associated him with a teddy bear: tall and wide, soft and cuddly. At the time, he was living in my mother's hometown of Adwa. My dad's younger sister Medhin hired a man to drive us there in an old, paint-chipped Toyota van. The journey was dangerous—we rode down winding mountainous dirt roads that had no guard rails. One wrong move and we would fall over the precipice into thick trees. When we finally arrived in Adwa, we pulled up to a small market area, poured out of the car, and waited for my uncle to arrive. I could tell by my mom's facial expression that she was growing annoyed. Then, my aunt Medhin pointed to a figure across the unpaved street. I buzzed with excitement at the chance to meet this man. As he came closer, I saw how his clothes draped on his small frame and realized that he was not much taller than my five-foot-four mother. The image I had of him disappeared, anxiety taking its place. It was only when he pulled me into an embrace that I felt an immediate connection to him. Despite being smaller than I expected, he was strong, holding me tight, kissing my cheeks multiple times. When he released me from his embrace, I realized that my imagination was not wrong.

My mother had not been back to Ethiopia for fourteen years by the time we went as a family in 2011. Within those fourteen years, she lost both her mom and an older brother, leaving her with an insurmountable amount of grief that was difficult to process alone in Canada. She would speak of them often and so it felt like they were near. But I could feel a heaviness filling the truck as we drove through Adwa toward her mother's house. My mom let out a guttural cry while the neighbours, who all knew my grandmother and helped raise my mom, surrounded her immediately, whisking her off into the house to calm her down. For me, there was a feeling of closure: they really were gone and, unlike with my Uncle Teddy, I would have to imagine what they might've looked like or how their hugs felt.

For a long time, my idea of "back home" was coloured by the stories my parents would tell us. My mom, who spent much of her young adulthood in the country's capital, zipping around town, could no longer tell you what was where. The different neighbourhoods had transformed. Many of the open-air marketplaces she went to as a young adult were now enclosed shopping areas and restaurants. At times, all my mom and dad could do was sit quietly in the back of the car, letting out a gasp every now and then at the changes around them. Their idea of "back home" disappeared. The skyline, previously open and clear, was now interrupted by the eruptions of tall condo buildings and factories. The conflict was apparent on their face; there was pride in the progress, but dismay that they could not recognize what was once their home.

Language was where I held most of my grief. Every time I met extended family, anxiety would cover me like an itchy blanket. The routine was the same: they would run up to hug my brother and me, plant multiple kisses on our cheeks and start speaking in rapid Tigrinya or Amharic to us. This collection of words—some I understood and some I did not—left me guessing what my family members were saying. It felt like a puzzle that I couldn't quite put together—a beautiful picture never fully realized. Despite my best efforts, my parents would have to come and translate what our family members were saying, even going so far as to help us respond in the appropriate language. However, when things got difficult, and I grew frustrated at how my English tongue couldn't wrap around a Tigrinya or Amharic word, I would respond in English and leave my parents to translate.

As you can imagine, my brother and I were slightly panicked when my parents left us with Howboy Haddish and Fita one day while they visited family members in a more dangerous part of Addis. We couldn't speak Tigrinya or Amharic and they couldn't speak English. *What do we talk to them about? Do we just stay in our rooms to avoid the awkwardness?* "We'll be back by lunchtime," our parents told us. Well, lunchtime came, and they were not back, leaving my brother and me to lie on the couch all day and watch Arabic MTV. That was until our aunt and uncle sat in the living room with us. Fita took the remote from the coffee table and changed the channel. Not wanting to spend an evening watching talking heads argue about politics, my brother and I sat up, ready to return to our rooms. "Kof belu, kof belu," my aunt and uncle said, waving their hands for us to sit back down. To our surprise, it wasn't the news that they were watching, but a World Wrestling Entertainment match. My brother and I glanced at each other as the theme music rolled in, shocked that the WWE was shown all the way in Ethiopia. Never having watched wrestling, we were both new to this world, but our aunt and uncle were experts, giving couchside commentary on the whole thing. Due to the language barrier, we all had to resort to visually expressing our thoughts to each other, and maybe, if lucky, use a word in the language the other party understood. If someone came up who they thought was going to win, my aunt would flex her arms to signal his strength and yell, "Good! Strong!" With every body slam they would cheer and applaud, even laugh at times, with my brother and I slowly following suit. By the time our parents finally did come home, they found all four of us yelling at the screen.

This was the first and last time I travelled to Ethiopia. Admittedly, I felt a wave of relief when we landed back in Toronto. We all did. Going "back home" was a logistical nightmare, with every day packed with meeting different family members, handing out items brought from Canada to the right people, and warding off family members who asked for a little too much. In September, I returned to school, feeling like I earned some sort of badge. I, too, could add to the conversation when the topic of "back home" came up. As I got older, I missed the country and planned on returning after receiving my undergraduate degree in 2020. I told myself this trip would be different. Instead of going on what my brother and I called the "royal tour," meeting family members and shaking hands, I would go to see specific sites. The obelisks in Axum. King Yohannes's palace in Mekelle. Unfortunately, 2020 brought with it a global pandemic and a war in Ethiopia. The latter changed my idea of "back home" forever. I began to see the dark underside of the country and it frightened me deeply. The beauty of Ethiopia that was recounted to me by relatives, the legends and history of that land, began to feel like buried treasures. But to reach them, you must wade through the country's muddier waters. Still, I long to return and experience Ethiopia for myself, to bridge the distance between myself and this faraway land.

ANGELO SANTOS

Shutter

A camera, to the uninitiated, is a grim contraption: it is covered in tiny buttons and dials, miniature switches and cold pieces of glass, and a rubbery black plastic like something lifted off the back of an orca. It feels bulky in your hands, an inert hunk of material. Recently, I saw an AI illustration of a professional camera and it looked monstrous: buttons crammed on every square inch of the camera's surface like a pox, the barrel of the lens choked with too many serrated rings, a few of which appeared to be melting into the rest of the camera. When Vi—my girlfriend then, now my wife—gave me my first real camera as a birthday gift, I remember feeling a twinge of foreboding while unboxing it, as though the machinery of the camera might get the better of me, fearful that perhaps someday I would get lost in its obscurities.

Still, when my cousin Vince asked me to be his best man at his wedding in Manila, I knew that I would take the camera with me. Besides being the country of my birth that my parents and I left when I was three, the Philippines was also the place where we as a family had returned to annually every summer for about a decade when we lived in the Middle East (where it was common practice to offer expatriate employees like my dad generous yearly vacation allowances as part of a standard benefits package); it was also the country that, now that we were in Canada, we hadn't visited for almost five years. My cousin's wedding aside, this was an occasion to bring a camera: a homecoming, a return to the motherland. Soon, my entire family was booked to make the pilgrimage: my parents, my two sisters (who were both born after we left the Philippines), and Vi, who was able to rearrange her work schedule to join us. For weeks leading up to the trip, I caught myself dreaming of halo-halo and inasal, tricycles and jeepneys, and the mellifluous iambic pentameter of spoken Tagalog on the streets.

Travelling with a camera, I soon learned, requires forethought and careful attention to detail. Before this trip, I had never carted along something so expensive, and I fretted over the prospect of damaging the camera at some juncture, opening my bag to find a cracked lens, or a rattle of internal components. I rearranged the padding in my carry-on so that the camera effectively stayed nestled in a cushion as we battled our way through the airport's long queues, as we wrestled our balik-bayan boxes onto flimsy baggage carts, and then as we sat and writhed through the punishing thirteen-hour flight to the other side of the world. When we emerged from the concourse doors into the oppressive tropical humidity of Manila, I checked inside the bag and was relieved to see that the camera was still intact. Vi, who had seen me peering into my carry-on several times over the course of the flight, teased, "Did our baby make it okay?" and I shot her back a dirty (but also guilty) look.

Months earlier, when the camera was still fairly new, Vi and I took a photography course in the cramped, dimly lit backroom of a local camera store in Toronto. We were drawn to the course because we had both been inspired by the pictures we saw on social media taken by accomplished photographers—the ones where the images looked sun-kissed, everyone's hair aglow, backgrounds blurred to a creamy texture—and we sought to recreate some of this magic on our own. Our instructor, an austere Scotsman whose work hung in galleries, had been insistent on imparting this particular strategy: memorize just a few of the most common settings, then just go out and shoot! "The trick is," he said, "not to let the camera get in the way." I scoffed at this advice, and promptly went home and scoured the Internet for hours, looking for the best tutorials. (Vi, who was more relaxed about things, was content to let me learn the basics first, then teach them to her later.) I read articles about aperture, shutter speed, and ISO; I watched videos about autofocus settings. Growing up, I was someone for whom anxiety about the unknown inspired bouts of intense overpreparation—this is what got me through school, after all—and I was not about to change this pattern of behaviour. All of this instruction coalesced in my mind into a murky, confusing tangle of numbers and concepts; at times, I felt as though it would be easier to build a camera from scratch than use one to take a decent picture. As my cousin's wedding approached, I secretly hoped that I might rise to the occasion, like the rookie who winds up at the free-throw line at the end of a tie game and calmly sinks a pair of baskets.

Unfortunately, once I actually got to the Philippines, all of that overpreparation did not pay off. This was not for lack of diligence; I took the camera everywhere: to the sprawling shopping malls patrolled by armed security guards, to the bustle of the local palengke, to the hotel with breathtaking views of Taal Volcano, to the restaurants where my family gathered for various pre-wedding celebrations. I snapped photos of colourful jeepneys in repose, posters of the Sacred Heart of Jesus plastered on lampposts, Vi smirking while holding the salacious man-in-a-barrel at a market. But after each day of shooting, I would remove the memory card from the camera to view the photos on my laptop's screen, and the results were sobering: most of the photos were some combination of too bright, too dark, or too blurry, and only about half were in focus. The only photos that were salvageable were the ones that I took in automatic mode, but these were also the photos that looked the most clinical, lacking that special magic that Vi and I wanted. I started to feel like I should consider putting the camera up for sale online.

My family, unaware of my crushed aesthetic aspirations (and conflating the possession of high-end photographic equipment with skill), were nonetheless thrilled with my new hobby; I instantly became the ad hoc family portraitist. I accepted my appointment with zeal; at least this way, I would get more practice. My services were enlisted at every gathering, every meal, every trip to the mall. To cope with demand, I eventually dispensed with my bag and started to wear the camera around my neck, the strap crossing my chest diagonally, allowing the camera to remain at my side like a holstered pistol, permanently wielded but still discreet enough not to draw too much unwanted attention (*The mandurukot will slice the strap in half when you're not paying attention and run away with your camera*, warned one of my cousins). Now, the moment someone uttered my clarion call—Kodakan tayo!—I was ready. Soon, I was filling entire memory cards with family portraits: photos of my relatives thronging at long tables at restaurants; my relatives thronging in the lobbies of upscale resorts; my relatives thronging in front of a mammoth karaoke machine at my uncle's house; my relatives thronging outside the nail salon for some pre-wedding pampering, Vi at the edge of the frame, trying her best to blend in with my boisterous aunts.

After the third week in the Philippines, I noticed it. Perhaps it was how the people at the market looked at me, or how their tone changed subtly when they addressed me. I had long been aware that there were differences in the way that I was treated compared to my relatives, but something had shifted, or perhaps I had just become more attuned to it. For this entire trip, I had taken pains to blend in; I wore nothing too extravagant or foreign, even opting for the most unassuming tsinelas and sandos from nearby shopping malls. But within seconds, everyone seemed to know the truth: I was an interloper, a non-local, and the camera was the icing on the cake. How could I have not seen it? I could not hide my accent, the halting way I spoke Tagalog, nor how I struggled to figure out exactly how to address someone on the street. And with this camera yoked around my neck, I was a walking caricature, a paparazzo, a Hawaiian tourist sans floral shirt. All this time, I was being recognized as an outsider, and this, I realized, was what produced that look that I was getting from everyone—a look that had undercurrents of fear and distrust, and at times felt slightly predatory, as though I were a commodity that could be exploited. Anyway, who could blame them, my kababayan? With my entry-level wage as a hospital physiotherapist in Toronto, I already had more money than most of them could dream of. Relatively speaking, I was the one with privilege, and in spades; at this point, I had already recognized my family back home as having privilege, but now I knew that, as a working balikbayan, I was in an echelon above. Nothing cemented this further than when I made a withdrawal from an ATM and saw my chequing account balance converted to Philippine pesos—if ever there was a time in my life that I felt the closest to being wealthy, it was then. What kind of world did we live in, that an hour of my labour in Canada could be worth so much more than an hour of someone's labour here?

At my cousin's wedding reception, in a swanky hall flanked on either side by extravagant floral displays, I gave my best man speech, a riff on how my cousin hoarded his toys as a kid. As I spoke, I remember thinking that *I* was the hoarder now, hoarding my attachments to this conception of the person I no longer was, a person with closer ties to my birth country than I actually had. In reality, my sense of belonging to the Philippines had been forfeited in a million tiny ways over the last few decades: when my dad emigrated as an overseas worker and took my mom and me with him when I was a toddler; when my parents chose to speak to me in English and not Tagalog; when my parents chose to send me to a school in the Middle East with an American curriculum—there were myriad other examples. And it wasn't my parents' fault; they did all of these things because they wanted to create better opportunities for me and my sisters. At the time, my parents were also caught up in something larger than themselves, namely the wave of migration in the 1980s spurred by dictator Ferdinand Marcos's move to create a remittance-based economy in the Philippines, a move that incentivized Filipinos to fill labour shortages all across the world, a move that profoundly and irrevocably changed the trajectory of all of our lives. Older now, I realize that sometimes we're all just flags in the wind, at the mercy of whatever gusts come our way.

As the dance music blared into the wee hours at the reception hall, one of my uncles asked me when I was coming back to the country to visit. I replied honestly that I didn't know, because I didn't feel like the same person who left years ago—and if this were the case, who would I even be when I came back? In that moment, I saw the years ahead of me: soon Vi and I would be forging a life of our own in Canada, apart from many of the Filipino traditions I grew up with, the traditions of my parents and grandparents, and those of their parents and grandparents. As much as I loved the Philippines, the truth was that it no longer felt like home to me, and neither for that matter did Canada nor the Middle East: I felt now edged into a new kind of rootlessness, and my home was one between countries, triangulated perhaps, in the middle of one of those vast blue oceans that we crossed on that airplane on the way here. I was—and probably would always be—overboard, adrift in the rolling waves.

The camera spent much of its time in my bag after that. I bristled whenever someone asked me for a photo, grunted in response if they asked again. On one of our last nights in Manila, possessed of a kind of wild energy, Vi and I brought the camera out and took photos of ourselves on the streets in my grandmother's barangay, giggling and posing outlandishly, trying to get the city lights softly out of focus in the background the way we saw in the photos we admired on social media. We took several dozen pictures of ourselves, both of us fiddling with the settings, but we could already tell by previewing the images on the camera's rear screen that night that none of them turned out—the images were all too dark and too grainy. "If you want to freeze a moment in time, you must get your shutter down to one-sixtieth of a second or less," our Scotsman instructor had enjoined us at the course, and I remember looking up helplessly at the images projected on the screen at that moment, images featuring blooms of water droplets frozen in time, a soccer player mid-kick with his leg thrust out, appearing as motionless as a statue.

I've kept all of the photos that Vi and I took that night, despite their obvious lack of quality. As it turned out, it would take us another full year or two before we truly felt competent at using that camera. Still, there is something intriguing to me about the imperfection of those photos: there are sixteen of me in total, and in every single one I am blurry, my edges not clearly delineated—I am in motion, forever unfrozen, the camera unable to capture me.

CHRISTINA HOAG

Dépaysement

French (n.): The removal from one's element, to be situated in unfamiliar surroundings.

Whenever I'm asked, "Where are you from?" my brain spins into an automatic checklist as to whether I answer with the long or short version of my life. Most of the time, I go with "New Jersey." That's the short version. Here's the long…

I should have been born in the remote copper-mining town of Mufulira in Zambia, where my father worked as an engineer. But when my mother, an English nurse at the mine hospital was about to give birth to me, Dad whisked her off to his home in New Zealand sheep country, and I entered the world.

A mere three weeks after my birth, we moved to Fiji for Dad's job at a gold mine. He was a shift boss, supervising the miners who worked underground. Then his career took us to Sweden, England, Nigeria, back to New Zealand, Australia, and finally New Jersey. All before my thirteenth birthday.

So, when people ask me, "Where are you from?" I don't have a straightforward answer. I have no homeland. Despite my passports from New Zealand, Australia, and the U.S., I feel no real claim to any country or nationality. Over the course of my life, I've been a chameleon, changing myself to belong wherever I am. Erasing old layers of myself to accommodate the new.

I became conscious of what's lost to moving countries—friends, daily routines, the familiarity of your surroundings—when we moved from New Zealand to Australia in late 1970. I was seven, deeply missing my ginger-haired best friend Janine, who I'd walk to school with every day, and my favourite doll, Patch, who somehow got lost in the move. I tried to recreate parts of my old life. In New Zealand, I walked with my sister to a church a couple of blocks away. Now I had to be driven, and my sister didn't go. I stopped attending after a couple of weeks, the only lesson I retained being that I ought to let the past dwell where it lives.

My brother, father, and I were Kiwis because we were born there; my mother and sister were born in Britain. Eventually, my parents got Australian citizenship so we would all carry the same passports instead of having a split-citizenship family. Later we added American passports to the collection.

At first, my younger siblings and I were excited. *America!* we thought. *Land of The Brady Bunch, Disneyland,* and *hamburgers!* We never thought of the differences that may exist beyond our TV-based knowledge. Americans couldn't understand our English. We had to repeat ourselves multiple times to shop assistants or gas attendants. At school, teachers were more accepting, but every time I opened my mouth in class, heads swivelled to see where this strange accent was coming from. Already shy, I wished to dissolve into the wall.

On top of that, I was ahead academically—a thirteen-year-old ninth grader trying to mingle with fifteen-year-olds way more advanced than me in their American teenagerdom. I had never owned a pair of Levi's or sneakers, hadn't even heard of a shopping mall. Teachers marked my British spellings as mistakes and struggled to read my handwriting because I'd learnt the Modern Cursive style used in Australia, with no tailed letters, r's that looked like printed r's and p's that resembled h's. I'd never seen snow or gone trick-or-treating. While I looked like any other white kid, I felt like an imposter.

With time, my accent and other Australianisms faded, and I became an American teenager indistinguishable from the others I grew up with. But in all that time, I still tried to cling to my old identity by writing to my Australian friends until my letters went unanswered. I gave every one of them a last chance, sending a final letter saying my last one must've gone missing in the post, but after the second letter yielded no replies, I had to accept that the thread had broken.

When we visited Sydney two years later, I thought I could finally be my true self. After all, this was home, or so said my passport. But everyone said I looked American, spoke like an American. The accent was about survival, I explained, a defence against being told "you talk funny" and asked to repeat myself, and being made to feel that my manner of speaking was more interesting than what I had to say.

The feeling deepened when I visited Australia a second time two years later. I was seventeen and in my first year at university. By then the country had adopted a new national anthem and the metric system. A new skyscraper lorded over Sydney, the needle-pointed Sydney Tower. I was now an Australian citizen turned American tourist.

I never returned to Australia after that trip. I came to the painful conclusion that I had to cut the mooring and let the Land of Oz drift into the ether of the distant past. So, if Australia—the country that I remembered the best, where I spent my formative childhood—wasn't home, then what was?

I decided to embrace being American, although I'd never learnt to sing "The Star-Spangled Banner" or eat a peanut-butter-and-jelly sandwich. I never mentioned growing up around the world and let everyone assume I was from northern New Jersey. I became the first in my family to get U.S. citizenship and begin the traditional American career climb, slogging for eight years as a reporter and editor at newspapers in northern and central New Jersey.

I got bored.

A yearning for novelty and adventure, no doubt seeded by my childhood, pushed within me. I couldn't keep pretending to be like my colleagues—content with covering small-town politics and school boards and vacationing at the Jersey Shore—because I wasn't. I quit my job with the abstract goal of living somewhere that would challenge me to learn another language, in the hope that I'd find my home in foreignness. Over the next decade, I moved from Spain to Guatemala to Venezuela, teaching English at times, but mostly working as a journalist for media in the U.S. and U.K.

I loved it. Every day presented a novelty, a chance to explore and learn.

What I didn't anticipate was that, although I was clearly foreign by my looks and my accent in Spanish, everyone assumed I was a typical American. But I wasn't. Nor was I really Australian or Kiwi. I was still adrift. Other lifelong nomads I met had grown up as children of diplomats, and thus their identity was anchored to their parents' country. It wasn't the same as how I was raised.

I grew to envy people who had hometowns, who grew up with sameness—the same kids, same house, same neighbours, same traditions. That stability seemed comforting, safe, nurturing. In my mid-thirties, I grew angry at my parents for hauling me around the world, for not giving me any constancy. I missed out on having meaningful ties with extended family. I'd never attended any of their weddings, christenings, or funerals. The angst and anger only lasted a matter of months. I was mature enough to realize that those feelings wouldn't get me anywhere. I couldn't change my nomadic upbringing. I had to accept it, stow it away again, move forward.

After ten years abroad, I returned to the United States, moving first to Miami, then to Los Angeles, where I remain. Unexpectedly, the similarities between California and Australia unearthed a host of childhood memories. A grove of eucalyptus trees with their bark peeling in huge curls to expose white trunks reminded me of a towering gum tree in our back garden in Sydney. The scent of wisteria transported me to the lavender vines that covered our neighbours' house where I'd breathe in the heady perfume. On a road trip to San Francisco, the hilly paddocks dotted with sheep touched a long-ago chord of road trips through New Zealand's South Island countryside to visit my uncle's farm. The memory swelled to an ache and tears trickled down my cheeks. California felt like a homecoming of sorts, looping my nomadic life as close as I could to my faraway childhood.

Far into middle age, I felt the unresolved question of my identity resurface. Now free of the youthful need to fit in, I thought I should be truer to myself, tell people the long version of my history instead of the version that starts in New Jersey. But that didn't last long. Ironically, I now received the skeptical remark, "But you don't have an accent." Or people would respond with a puzzled stare and change the topic. Two guys even accused me of making up my international childhood. I felt compelled to pronounce a few words with an Australian accent to prove I was telling the truth. I couldn't win.

I needed to find other people who grew up moving around the world. I had met only a few throughout my life. Surely, there had to be more. I searched the Internet, and I found them.

To my surprise, we have a name: third-culture kids, or TCKs, which represents that we are raised in a "third place," out of our birth countries or the cultures of our parents. We are most often children of diplomats, military personnel, missionaries, or multinational corporate employees.

I found a body of studies and literature about TCKs. The irony is that every TCK has a unique journey, even among siblings. Since I am the eldest, I have lived in three more countries than my sister, for example. Yet TCKs share many characteristics. We are easily bored, adaptable, flexible, broad-minded. People who grew up as TCKs tend not to have strong opinions on issues because we can see all sides. We appreciate difference rather than judge it.

We also face the same issues and challenges. The lifelong feeling of being a square peg trying to fit into a round hole. The restlessness. Who to root for during the Olympic Games and the World Cup. Not having childhood friends in adulthood or relationships with extended family. The eternal dilemma of not having a home, of not belonging.

In adulthood, some TCKs never really settle down. They continue moving and travelling. That's me. Others eschew that lifestyle altogether and deliberately stay put. That's my sister. My TCK childhood made me unafraid to venture into the unknown, to travel to remote places. It has made me aware and curious about how people live in other parts of the world, and appreciative of what I have.

For the first time, I felt that my life made sense. I had found my community at last.

EUFEMIA FANTETTI

Where the Bodies Are Buried

BACKBONE

Here are the ruminations that obsessed me whenever I thought of returning for a visit to Bonefro, the ancestral Italian village: who would welcome me, and which relatives could shun me? What am I willing to divulge about myself or my life? When should I reveal my travel plans? Where might I find safe havens? Why did I feel the need to prepare explanations and excuses?

After the rancorous union and eventual rift between my parents, I stayed away for thirty-six years and assumed welcome mats soaked in lighter fluid and lit on fire the moment I set foot in the area. The relationship status between me and la bel paese was complicated. Two ships passing in the night—the Titanic and the Lusitania.

My earliest memories marinate in Molise, the region where Bonefro is situated. I spent a long winter there when I was five, attending Mass, eating roasted chestnuts, meeting and visiting extended family. Liqueurs (Marsala, anisette, and Zabov) were pulled out and poured into cordial glasses that perfectly fit into my tiny hands. As an adult, I told everyone, "Italians give their kids liquor to soften the blow of childhood." My second trip occurred over the opposite season, a summer when I was still a child, eleven years old. Tasked with watching over my mother's treatment for psychosis, I ended up pitched in a battle of wills against my maternal grandmother, the Grande Dame of sociopaths. I lost—arguments, items of clothing, respect for almost everyone linked to me by blood—and left Italy never planning to return.

Reaching out to a few friends about my fears, I asked for talismans, anything that could protect me on the journey. I suggested good luck charms, favourite poems, meaningful quotes, images of deities or holy individuals. I received semi-precious gemstones, a rock from an Ontario riverbed, a gorgeous pen, and a prayer specifically for journeyers. I wanted to inoculate myself before travelling to the hot zone of anguish, regret, and trauma.

I set some intentions: 1) don't bring shame to the family; 2) don't bring shame to the family; 3) don't bring shame to the family. Technically, at the time of this trip as a twice-divorced, single woman in her forties who flirted with Buddhism, I'd already failed in this endeavour. But then I comforted myself with horror stories about my mother's mother, played back memories of Nonna Sapooch's outlandish cruelty and my own mother's epic inability to parent and decided shame is as shame does. Besides, I thought, let's not kid myself. Born into a misogynist, patriarchal, Roman Catholic culture that lionized males and villainized females, the odds were stacked, Jenga-style, against me. Without glossy hair, perfect body proportions, saintly behaviour, a willingness to be subservient to someone else's needs, and a delicious ragu to rival others and serve to any guest any time, beatification was not my future. I can handle the disappointment; some days I even juggle the rejection: living life on my own terms outside of a conformist society—the birthplace of fascism, where the populace recently voted a far-right party into power and propagandist belief is summed up in the saying, "Mussolini also did a lot of good"—is a win any way I slice the Panettone.

FUNNY BONE

It's wrong to call Bonefro a village. In Italian, it's a comune of slightly over a thousand people (reduced from five thousand plus in pre-diaspora days). Comune translates into municipality—though it's jarring to think of a hillside settlement of 1,200 people in a rural setting as a city. For years, the false cognate of commune, a term I learned first in English, did not fit the locale by any stretch of my imagination. I can't match the thousand-year-old castle, the eight-hundred-year-old (rebuilt) Santa Maria delle Rose Church, or the four-hundred-year-old Santa Maria delle Grazie former convent with images I associate with lifestyle choices and the scent of sandalwood. There are many words my mental dictionary won't translate, Bonefro remains "the village" in all my recounting.

Part of this messy inner monologue spills out to the customs agent at Rome's airport, in rusty pronunciation hampered by Inglese-influenced dialect.

His head tilted at an angle to study me. "Really? You haven't been to visit your relatives here in thirty-six years?"

I nodded. "Imagine the guilt."

He smiled and stamped my passport. "Welcome back."

Nadia, a friend from Rome whom I met when I lived in Vancouver, picked me up. She would be my host, tour guide, and, fortunately, transportation to Bonefro. Sixteen years and a handful of emails had passed before we reunited. Relief flooded through my heart when she embraced me in a fierce hug. *Perhaps*, I let myself think, *the days ahead could be curative.* I'd piggybacked this trip onto a writers' conference in Padula, Salerno, where I was scheduled to participate on two panels that Nadia was game to attend. Her folks lived in Campobasso, the capital of Molise, twenty-five kilometres southwest from ground zero.

Through Facebook, I connected with my maternal cousin's daughter to let them know the day I would arrive. Nadia lives by a different clock. My jaw tensed at our late morning departure. Nadia sped down the motorway while I chewed my inner cheek, unable to admire the cloudless azure canopy above.

An hour later, on the outskirts of the village, Nadia stopped and pointed to the Bonefro sign above the posted speed limit of thirty. We parked across from Luisa's home, in front of a building that turned out to be the seniors' home where my paternal grandfather Gennaro lived out his days, a short walk from the piazza—the town square—core meeting place of elderly men in every Italian municipality.

At eleven, I was chastised for walking through the piazza in mid-day and entering a café-slash-bar-slash-man-cave to buy myself a ghiacciolo, a lemon popsicle with a licorice stem. Nonno Gennaro interrupted his card game, pulled me outside, and explained the etiquette I'd overlooked. A girl walking around in shorts and a halter top was problematic enough, he noted, but in the middle of the day? The impropriety of walking into an espresso bar. The indecency of asking for another sweet. If I wanted ice cream, I should curb my appetite and ask him to purchase one for me. Good girls were labouring at home during the day, not broadcasting their laziness in search of gelato. In Canada, I was a shy, quiet, well-behaved kid. My face flushed with embarrassment from my grandfather's reprimand. The message: me being myself, doing my own thing—was intolerable. Survival in this inhospitable clime seemed linked to the rejection of my identity and individuality. My parents—through their own immersion in urban life—forgot customs and neglected the rules of engagement for a girl.

Luisa greeted us with a kiss on both cheeks. She introduced her husband, teenaged daughter, and son. Over a table laden with cold cuts and Provolone cheese plus plates piled high with penne in a tomato sauce, she kept offering Coca-Cola, Fanta, and wine. I declined, marvelling at the fact that I was drinking fresh water from a Bonefran fountain. Crystal clear, Bonefro's famous spring water sparkled under the Mediterranean sun. A primal element deeply intertwined with my ancestors' survival, I thirsted after the restorative liquid and waved off wine.

"This is the first time in a lifetime I can drink the same water our ancestors drank."

Luisa glanced at Nadia and eyed me with interest. "I wonder. Why didn't you turn to our grandmother for help?"

I shot an incredulous glance across the table and weighed my options. Insult now or wait and draw my "Don't bother to talk about events you don't understand" attitude across the duration of my visit? I ran my tongue across my teeth as I returned her gaze and chose a modified Door Number 1.

"Sapooch was not a person who could help." The height of my self-control (and kindness) included not shouting "Nonna was a devil-spawned beast." I stopped from listing how intensely our grandmother made matters worse, frequently goading her daughter, my mother, into full-blown psychotic rages over the phone and insisting Mamma had married beneath herself.

Luisa stayed firm. "I don't know. I remember when your mother visited for the grandparents' fiftieth wedding anniversary, and she came downstairs dressed inappropriate for the weather. Her oldest sister, Zia Nicolina, told her to go upstairs and change and she did. In my opinion, your mom was capricious."

Jesus H. Christ. I mean, Gesù Acca. Cristo.

Nadia politely ignored the discussion and heaped another serving of salad on her plate.

"Capricious doesn't explain all the police visits to our home. Her shoplifting. Her violence. Her assaults on her sister-in-law and the nurse at my father's factory. Capricious? You mean *crazy*. If we're going to talk about this at all, I won't accept any other words."

This position became my refrain, repeated with Zia Nicolina, and Zi' Antonio, Luisa's father and my mother's older brother. I persisted with cousins from both sides. By the time a stranger approached with invasive curiosity to ask, "Are you speaking with your mother?" I was snarky, turning to another relative, my father's cousin Gina with my reply: "Don't people have televisions here? Or is the telenovela of my mother's mental illness still the most entertaining story?"

On the drive back to Campobasso, Nadia asked how I felt.

"Exhausted." Eyes shut, I slumped in the passenger seat, drained from translating terms and manoeuvring ignorance. No one ever wanted to admit that mental illness ran in the family. I'd navigated through denials, disavowals, and suspicions of demonic possession since my early teens. I didn't burn bridges with the family, I carpet-bombed them, cutting multiple relatives out of my life, including my severely ill mother. At the time of the trip, I hadn't spoken to her for three years. She was gangrenous flesh needing to be excised from my life. Clearly, some villagers still gossiped through the grapevine about my nuclear family. I could hear their condemnations: *What kind of daughter abandons a sick mother who can't speak the language? This is what happens when children are raised Canadian—they lose all sense of family.*

WISHBONE

Luisa studied my manicured hands and pedicured feet saying, "I've never done that." She'd been a young bride and now, a doting mother. She's skittish about the refugee crisis (the number of asylum-seekers sweeping through Lampedusa in 2016 are staggering and heartbreaking). I countered: for a country with a diaspora the size of Italy's to deny shelter to those in search of peace and potential prosperity is criminal and inhumane. As a kid, I adored her and preferred her company to anyone else's, but then I reasoned that her older brother was a bully and her youngest brother, still a baby.

Over lunch she voiced a daydream that I would fix up my father's home—damaged in the 2002 earthquake—and spend summers in Molise. "What do you think? Is it possible?"

Her husband chimed in to say the government no longer funded the rebuild.

I contemplated an alternative life. One where I could live the stereotype of Italian connectivity, holding huge feasts for family and friends, inviting everyone to stay for free in an idyllic setting straight from a Renaissance painting. I coveted the seductive surroundings—the emerald hills, golden wheat fields, and mackerel sky formation against turquoise as if God airbrushed the clouds himself.

The ache in my chest was that ancient longing to belong that thrums through the heart of humanity. We cannot survive without others. Even hermits know this, I'm sure. I visualize the venture: the ability to visit and tend to the graves of my beloved Nonna Femia and Nonno Gennaro whenever I wanted. To plant plums in the soil that fed my ancestors for a millennium and more. To eat fresh figs, to run into second, third, and fourth cousins during a stroll, to speak the language of Dante, flawlessly greeting everyone without dread lodged in my throat.

Could I collect all the sensory story details I desired then? I wondered.

I'd prepped a bucket list for this trip: visit the Capuchin Crypt, tour the Colosseum, take in a museum or art gallery. A bout of heatstroke sidelined all plans. I managed to observe a sunrise in Molise, the hills in the distance glowing pale yellow and tangerine. Once I regained partial strength after several incoherent and painful days stuck in bed, I joined a tour group making its way through the crowded iconic amphitheatre.

And my favourite memory: After lunch, as Luisa and her daughter accompanied me and Nadia on a walk, my cousin spoke of the quake that structurally destroyed parts of the old village. Her kids were in school when the ground shook at eleven on October 31.

I was about to say "Halloween," when Nadia spoke up. "The Day of the Ancestors."

"Right before All Saints," Luisa added.

Steadily we marched at an incline of forty-five degrees until Luisa stopped and said, "Is something calling to you? Do you feel anything?"

I glanced at the pale pink, dilapidated three-storey structure on the corner and gasped. "It's the house!"

"It's your house—"

I corrected her. "—it's my father's." I ran to the locked street-level stable where chickens, pigs, and rabbits were raised. A yoke hung on the wall next to a rusted bicycle. A wooden ladder led to the main floor of the house—the trap door to the main floor lay open.

A woman drew near as I snapped pics with trembling hands. She lived across the road, a paved pathway of about three metres. She'd known my nonna and cried out, "You look exactly like Zi Femia!"

Luisa asked, "Where is everyone? Hoped we'd catch Frank." Luisa thought my father's delinquent cousin who lived in the adjacent abode had a key.

"A serpent passed by this morning. Everyone's inside with their doors closed."

Someone found someone with a bolt cutter to pry open the gate. A man of slight build entered through the animal stall and unlocked the front door. Everyone insisted I not cross the threshold—too perilous. Thirty years of dust caked the photos and furniture. A propane tank stood off to the side of the stove. The walls contained massive fissures angled like trapped lightning. Rubble was strewn across my grandparents' bed. The man retrieved my grandfather's army portrait, First Communion photos of my cousins, and a wedding portrait of my parents that I hadn't seen since their acrimonious divorce a decade earlier.

Back in Campobasso, I carefully cleaned the glass frames, my hands turning black from grime.

Tongue tired and mind depleted, in English I asked, "Nadia, a snake in front of the house on Via Rosello. What do serpents represent?" In Christianity, the molting creatures are affiliated with evil. As a boy, my father narrowly avoided death by viper; the family dog, Rizzoli, barked a warning, leapt in front of my dad, and died from the venomous bite. I was open to the possibility the presence was an auspicious sign, an off-beat welcome.

Nadia thought it over. Exhaling cigarette smoke she said, "Knowledge. They represent knowledge."

How fortuitous. Understanding was what I wanted all along. This trip was only the beginning.

SEEMA DHAWAN

Coriander, Chai, and Canada

It's impossible to go back where I came from, because where I came from came with me. It's in the black tea leaves I drop into my pot of water every morning, the charred liquid boiling chai as pieces of cardamom flip over. It's in the fact that I know that the stem of coriander has the most flavour and never discard it from my cutting board, as if it were trash. It's in the way I stood up for my Grade 8 classmate when he was being bullied in my new Canadian school, my bold Mumbai personality seeping through.

At the same time, a part of where I came from was left behind. It's the Arabian Sea that calls to me, feeling imbalanced by my removal, wondering where I am. It's the flat in Mumbai, vacant just for a beat before a new family furnished it with new dreams, its floors still adjusting to the new movements above.

It took me a total of sixteen years to get over my parents' decision to move us from a city of thirty-five million to Calgary, a city with far fewer inhabitants than yearly visitors to the Taj Mahal.

I vowed to return to India. I looked for all types of excuses and opportunities to go back, from volunteering and exchange programs to summer vacations and job opportunities. I thought if I got an impressive enough job in India, then I would simply have to move. When I was twenty-three, I applied for jobs and was called by a recruiter. "It says your education is from Canada?" he asked, confused by my application.

"Yes," I said.

"But you live in India now?"

"Kind of. I can move to India immediately," I said.

"Ah, okay," he said; I never got a call back.

Six months later, after a visit to Mumbai, I found myself lounging in Chhatrapati Shivaji Maharaj International Airport, reflecting on my love for this city. There was something about its rhythm, about its *homeness*, that instantly picked me up in its joy, making me want to stay.

As I sat there, waiting to board my flight, begrudging yet another departure, it hit me: I had just graduated from university and I had paid my dues by giving this "living in Canada" thing a chance. Why don't I just try to get a job here, rent a flat, and see how it goes?

Suddenly, leaving seemed like the most irrational thing to do. I called my mom, convinced I was about to make the wrong choice by getting on the plane. "Are you sure it is a good idea for me to get on this flight?" I asked her. "What am I even waiting for?"

My mom tried to reason with me. "Get the job and then you can go back," she said.

But I reasoned back: how will I get a job if I'm in Canada? It's always easier for companies to hire locals. "Why don't I just get an apartment and see how it goes for a few months?" I said.

"Do you know how much an apartment costs in Mumbai?"

I conceded that I should plan this out better, then I boarded the flight, but not before buying two extra vada pavs, just in case it would take me extra time to taste my favourite street food again.

It wasn't until my visit to India six years later, while sitting in the back of a black-and-yellow taxi in Mumbai, that I looked around the city and, for the first time in my life, I didn't feel an urgent need to stay.

I still felt at home and an overwhelming sense of love for the city, but I also felt a strange sense of acceptance with living elsewhere. To this day, I don't know what caused me to finally relax. Maybe it was because my surroundings were different for so many years by this point, that the tall trees and Gothic buildings of Mumbai felt removed from my everyday life. Maybe it was because I now found that I missed Canadian things in India, while still missing India in Canada.

A few years later, I had my first opportunity to visit India for work. Invited to a tourism conference in Goa, I quickly befriended a few foreign journalists. One of them asked some of the tourism representatives if they had any accommodation recommendations for Mumbai, the city we were headed to next. The representatives assumed that the journalists were looking for complimentary accommodations. Speaking to each other in a local dialect I can understand, they warned against making any promises to these journalists. I chuckled to myself, realizing they thought of me as a foreigner, too, or at least as someone too severed from her Indian origins to understand the local dialect.

Being between homes means you're always adapting and merging between cultures, making a new home of your own so much so that, at times, even the locals can't spot you.

I once asked the owner of an Indian restaurant in Calgary, "Don't you ever want to go back?" This was something I asked often, curious about why others hadn't moved back yet.

"Canada is a sweet beehive," she said. Sticky, sweet, entangling. "Once you come here, you stay," she added as she filled a cardboard container with laddus.

Going back to India now is bittersweet. The Arabian Sea still calls to me, and seeing familiar faces on the street makes me feel at home. Yet, while my favourite sweet shops are still there, my grandparents who bought the laddus for me aren't. The streets are busy, but the homes are emptier. I could join the workforce, more easily than ever, but am not sure if my values would fit in. I'm entangled in the beehive. There's the sweetness of Canadians, a country whose apologetic demeanour I've come to adore. There's the stickiness that often arises when I smell some marigolds, or bite into a soft piece of naan, of wanting to move to India, but wanting to stay in Canada more. There's the entanglement of loving my life in Canada now, like wearing an outfit that fits really well, but never fully.

So I make chai in the mornings, boiling those tea leaves until they've given it their all, and then sit back and relish all the good parts of the move, of which there are many. We can never fully go back to where we came from, but isn't that always true for everyone?

OFELIA BROOKS

Find Your Way Back

> Your mother tongue is your window into the world.
> —Ngũgĩ wa Thiong'o, *Between the Covers* podcast

"Will you go to Belize with me?" I asked my mother while she made panades in her kitchen. I had a free summer before starting law school. Friends had invited me on trips to Belize during spring break, but I always declined. I'd never been and couldn't go without my mother, who was all I knew about the country my family had emigrated from in the seventies, thirty years before I asked her to take me there.

She raised her eyebrow and returned to the panades. She scooped tuna out of a can onto a disk of masa. "Mek Ai tink bowt dat," she said in Kriol, Belize's mother tongue. *Let me think about that.*

Nobody talked about going back to Belize when I grew up in California in the nineties. While many immigrants longed to return home if only for a visit, my family did not. My family came to the States to get green cards, not visas. They wanted to be, and became, permanent residents.

They looked forward. Returning to Belize was going in the wrong direction. Back to a crowded two-bedroom cottage. Back to working in grade school to afford necessities. Back to military turmoil, as the colony fought for its independence from the U.K., and the attendant sexual violence by soldiers that was the price of self-determination.

My mother waited a week before my first trip to tell me she couldn't go. "Ai chrai bot Ai noh deh eena di rait main fi goh deh," she admitted. *I tried, but I'm not in the right mind to go there.*

She had no desire to revisit the chaos she had barely escaped.

Disheartened, I told her I'd go alone and stay with distant relatives.

She dropped me at the airport. I hugged her and whispered, "I hope you'll be able to go back one day."

I guzzled the thick air as I walked toward the Philip Goldson International Airport terminal. While other passengers choked on the humidity, my lungs seemed to have breathed this air before.

A cab ride later, I tapped on my grand-aunt's house door. A younger version of my grandmother answered. She welcomed me into a living room with people resembling my mom and her siblings. Same Indigenous almond eyes, coarse hair, and clay-red undertones. Same mestizo coils, freckles, and endless eyelashes. Same Creole high cheekbones and mahogany skin.

They hurried me to the couch and peppered me with questions. I answered in English. They looked puzzled and asked more questions in Kriol. With with each of my responses in English, their excitement faded.

I reassured them I could understand Kriol. I just couldn't speak it. "How dat mi hapn? Yu da noh Bileezyan?" they asked. *How did that happen? Aren't you Belizean?*

I exhaled as my grand-aunt called us to the table, relieved that I would not have to find an answer to those particular questions. I heaped spoonfuls of stewed chicken, rice and beans, salad, and plantains on my plate while I let the breezy, melodic Kriol around the table lull me away. I poked a cousin for more plantains.

"Now wat da 'plan-tain?'" he imitated my phonetic pronunciation of 'plantain.' "Da plaan-tin," he corrected, shortening the last syllable where I had elongated it.

The table laughed about those da farain—*foreigners*. I shrunk in front of people who may have looked identical to me, but were strangers.

It was time to learn Kriol. I needed to figure out where to begin.

My grandmother spoke Kriol with her children while they raised my generation in the States, but they didn't teach us how to speak it. They locked Kriol away.

For most of the country's history, Belizeans called their language "Broken English." They were taught that Kriol, their native tongue, was inferior to European colonial languages. It was considered a degenerate version of English that originated with enslaved Africans who mixed up their native African languages with English when speaking to their captors. Belizeans were banned from speaking Kriol outside the home, whether the home was in Belize or elsewhere. In my household in the States, Kriol had no place.

Since Kriol would have no role in my success in the U.S., I never asked to learn to speak it. By the time I realized it wasn't a bastardized version of English, but rather was a full-fledged language of its own, I was away in college on the East Coast, and it was too late to practice speaking it at home.

My classmates knew me as a Black girl from California. Only when people questioned if I was "regular Black" did I reveal that I was Central American.

A Central American identity was as specific as I got until a student in history class said Belizeans were the same as Jamaicans. I chimed in, "No. We're our own people with our own culture."

My friends gave me quizzical looks and fired off questions.

"You're from Belize?"

"What are people from Belize called?"

"Aren't y'all Spanish or something?"

"Are you related to Shyne?"

I answered most questions. But when I shared that one of the languages spoken in Belize was Kriol, and they motioned for me to say something, I didn't even attempt. I couldn't do it.

Not being able to speak the language made me feel like a fake. But Kriol reminded me of the heritage from which I was estranged, of the past my family left.

So, I put it away. I stayed silent during future academic discussions about Caribbeans.

My grandmother passed away during the COVID-19 pandemic. My siblings and I begged my mother to go to Belize with us and her grandchildren. She obliged us, not wanting her grandkids to miss out on going to Belize with their grandmother as we had.

It had been fifty years since my mother had set foot in Belize. We stayed in a hotel in Belize City, the country's capital, where my family was from. My mom didn't talk much. She waved off the constant questions about what it was like to return, what was different, and what was the same.

She had no clue. She had blocked out her traumatic life in Belize.

I tried to lift her spirits by suggesting visiting the main street she grew up on. Tall grass covered the lot where her childhood house once stood. City officials had torn it down to make way for a cemetery. I looked at the lot blankly. I had never been there or seen pictures. I had nothing to miss.

After the trip, I prodded my mother about the next one. She cut me off. She would never go back.

Returning to the motherland with my own mother didn't show me where I belonged. The family home was a graveyard. There was nothing to miss.

One of my aunts organized a family reunion in the house we grew up in for my grandmother's first heavenly birthday. Only the family matriarch could get all fourteen of us together. As many immigrants from developing countries do, we lived packed together in a small house in California until a family fight turned into a two-decades-long fissure beginning in 2000. All of the adults except an aunt moved out with their children in tow while my grandmother and aunt stayed in the family home.

I looked around the room, wondering how we had gotten here. The guests checked their phones. An hour had passed, and we were past the distraction of food and pleasantries.

The host, my aunt Vanessa, turned the television to YouTube. She started to input letters in the search bar.

I could bet what was coming. Only one song was played nonstop in the house before the family split. "Nani Wine," a soca classic, was my grandmother's favourite. The fast, percussive beat would summon the family to wherever my grandmother was to dance and sing along. I looked at Vanessa askance, unsure if the song would retain its magic.

A few aunts and uncles tapped their feet when "Nani Wine" blared. Vanessa noticed. She teased over the noise, "Ai si yu memba dehnya sang." *I know you remember these songs.* "Memba dehndeh dayz da Bileez wen wi mi-di daans ahn sing ahn wain ahn ting?" she said while following the song's instructions and twisting her waist like it was wire. *"You remember the days in Belize when we used to dance, sing, wine, and stuff,"* she said.

My aunts and uncles stood up and bobbed their heads one by one. Before too long, my generation stepped to the middle of the room and swayed to the beat.

My mother eventually joined the crowd and blurted the chorus, "Nani wain dong low. Nani wain dong soh."

Kriol's rhythm was buried deep. It was time to resurrect it.

I scoured the Internet for a Kriol tutor. Unlike mainstream languages, Belizeans only heard Kriol at home. Newscasters didn't speak in it, journalists didn't write in it, and teachers didn't teach it in school. There were no Google translations, movies with Kriol subtitles, or Rosetta Stone compact discs.

Fortunately, I found Kriol classes offered online by a mid-fifties cab driver living in Belize City. I started weekly classes on Skype. I learned words of the day, proverbs, and syntax in class on social media as I followed Belizean missives about appropriate slang for someone my age, classic songs any prideful Belizean knew by heart, and how to flirt, joke, and curse in Kriol.

I loved the way Kriol sounded. I adored its melodic lilt, bombast, and mixture of English, Spanish, Garifuna, and Mayan influences.

My interest in learning Kriol amused my mother. Apparently, I had been ashamed of it as a child. She reminded me, "Yu mi seh wee mi-di taak foni." *You said we spoke funny.*

Perhaps the shame my mother perceived was because I couldn't talk Kriol back to my grandmother when she asked me how school was, or boast during a rowdy family game of Po-Ke-No. I'd sigh out an answer in English. As I learned Kriol as an adult, I stopped referring to it as Broken English. There was nothing broken about our language to me.

Late into the reunion, past my mother's fake dinner plans if things got awkward, we said goodbye.

How would I connect to my family and country as time passed after my grandmother's death? I couldn't recount old memories—I had only a few. I couldn't just listen to soca songs—I didn't know many of those, either. There was no nostalgia to grasp. Those from destroyed homes aren't homesick.

I remembered a YouTube video from Kriol class. Two Belizean girls teach Kriol slang. One introduces the phrase "gaahn awf." The other explains: "If your friends played in a game well, you tell them, 'Unu gaaahn awf!'" The girls, more mestizo than Vanessa and my mom, sounded like them. In my mind, I saw Vanessa and my mom playing in the grassy yard of the cottage, high-fiving the other after winning Po-Ke-No. "Wee gaahn awf pahn dat!" my mother cheers.

In another video, a Belizean fashion designer explains Kriol sayings. She looks to be in her twenties, the same age my grandmother was when she left Belize.

The fashion designer introduces the next phrase: "When someone looks nice, we say 'Yu noh eezi.'" She stretches out the first syllable of the Kriol word for 'easy.' Eeeeee-zi. I heard my grandmother saying Yu noh eeeeee-zi to my mother, twirling in a frilly dress my grandmother sewed. My mother goes to the school dance. "Nani Wine" booms. She puts her long fingers over her button nose and full lips while she wain dong low. I could imagine her because she gave me the same features. She was not easy at all.

Through Kriol, I could go back. I could go to places I'd never been and see things where I never was. By speaking the language kept only for family, I could gain a piece of the identity for which I'd yearned. I could go home.

I recently called my mother out of the blue. She answered in English.

I cleared my throat and relaxed my tongue into saying, "Gud maanin. Wats op?"

Her pause worried me. Maybe she needed to be in the mood for language practice. She spoke Kriol for my sake, but returning home was challenging. She had to be in the right mind.

Then she spilled, "Oah gyal Ai fain. Laad, mek Ai tel yu wat mi hapn di ada day." *Girl, I'm fine. Lord, let me tell you what happened the other day.*

Her voice lightened. I heard her reach a part of herself that had been distant for too long. She was back dancing and playing under the Belizean sun.

Her ease put me at ease. I answered, without as much effort as in Kriol class, "Gyal, mek shoar yu tel mee evriting!" *Girl, make sure you tell me everything!*

She giggled while gossiping about her neighbours. I baited her for more dirt in almost perfect Kriol.

Sometimes, the voyage home is a different path than imagined.

Through Kriol, I am finding the way back. For my mother. And for me.

JUNE CHUA

Foreign Body

My sisters and I had been walking toward the washroom, a small concrete building standing several metres away from my great-aunt's home in Kuching. It was our first day in Malaysia and our family's first trip to the motherland since migrating to Canada eight years prior, when I was six. We were unaccustomed to the idea of having to pee into chamber pots, and so we plotted to go together.

On our way, we saw an elderly gardener tending to the plants before he left for the day. He'd quickly assessed us and muttered: "Oh, the Australians!" My great-aunt's grandchildren, who lived in Australia, sometimes visited. They looked very different from us, as their mother had a European background.

So, we thought we fit in.

That, perhaps, we looked like we belonged.

His statement immediately cast us as outsiders.

"No, we're from Canada. But how did you know we aren't from here?" my older sister asked.

"You smell like butter!" And with that, he shuffled off. His words cloaked the air. It was so humid and hot, I felt like sticky rice wrapped in banana leaf. Now, I imagined myself as a melting stick of butter.

We had been in Canada for seven years by then. Somehow, Canada had infused us with a milky smell that emanated foreignness no matter what we looked like. Physiological transformations were afoot.

I have since discovered that in parts of East Asia, Westerners are thought to reek of butter. In post–World War II Japan, when it was heavily occupied by American and British Allied Forces, foreigners were deemed bata-kusai, a derogatory term meaning "stinking of butter."

When we first arrived in Canada in the seventies, people offered us giant glasses of milk and cheeseburgers, or—worst of all—milkshakes! We could barely finish half of the shakes, the milk, the burgers. They gave us stomach aches and seemed faintly disgusting to taste—the odour of cow's milk was peculiar, like inhaling the stench of a farm. The cold liquid winding its way down our digestive tracts felt thick and heavy, the sludgy milkshakes lining the walls of my stomach like house paint.

In Malaysia, evaporated milk and sweetened condensed milk were staples like rice or shrimp paste. In tropical lands, canned foods were safe to keep for months. It was rare to get cakes with whipped cream as the heat would render them a sodden mess within minutes.

When we first arrived in Canada, we soon began our journey of ingesting many more milk-based foods, which in time became an intrinsic part of our diet. It was converting me on a cellular level, altering my being. A Canadian friend once told me how simple it was to make butter; you just whip the cream until the fat separates from the liquid. I immediately thought of myself as the cream and the force of migration as the mixer, separating me into something new and shapeable.

CAKE

I turned seven a month after our arrival. Dad traversed a busy Vancouver freeway to purchase a Black Forest cake from Safeway. We thought the name of the supermarket odd but liked that it conferred a greeting—*welcome, you will be secure here.* From that point on, this utterly

German confection would be the only cake we'd ever have for birthdays. Mum was obsessed with it. She loved the layers of cherry-liquored cream interspersed with chocolate cake and topped with maraschino cherries. It was mostly cream. Those cakes tasted of fake milk product and bad, syrupy liqueur. I think it perhaps represented all those European-style cream cakes she could never get back home. Nevertheless, it became tradition. A new ritual to signify our march toward citizenship and a frosted future.

In time, we were complaining to my mom whenever she cooked curry or stir-fried veggies with fermented shrimp paste, telling her that belacan stank like stinky socks.

It made our clothes and hair reek, we said. Not wanting this foreign smell to block our integration, we urged her to only cook her Malaysian/Chinese dishes on weekends. We still hankered for those flavours from time to time.

MAC 'N' CHEESE

My older sister was tasked with making us after-school snacks and lunches during spring and summer breaks. This meant an array of convenience foods: lots of mac 'n' cheese, creamy Campbell's soups, canned Chef Boyardee ravioli, and in warm months, ice cream. Our fridge was stocked with those orangey slices of cheese in their clear sleeves. I recall peeling off the cheese tile as a quick after-school snack. In the mornings, I enjoyed the saccharine sweetness of the milk in my Cap'n Crunch. I devoured Fudgsicles and Peanut Buster Parfaits at the Dairy Queen in my neighbourhood.

We were slowly transforming from the inside, upping our intake of cottage cheese and yogurt. Each morsel of milky food was immersing us further into Western culture and habits. It would be irreversible. Moreover, my parents had instituted an English-only rule, afraid that we'd fall behind in school. They didn't imagine the consequences of severing our linguistic connection, that one day we'd return to Malaysia, and, without Hokkien, find it impossible to communicate with our aunties, uncles, and cousins. We were to become milk-fed, Anglo-adjacent Canadians in order to succeed in one of five approved professions: doctor, lawyer, dentist, engineer, or corporate leader with an MBA. Our monolingual status would help us get there, just another part of Western culture that we were to inhabit like an ill-fitting costume.

Yet, externally, we were still so different from the mainstream population. Children often made fun of our eyes, pulling the sides of their eyes to become slanted. Our Western "costume" was transparent.

I longed to have eyelids and paler skin.

I was a yellow alien with slitted eyes...

...capped by thick, black hair that absorbed the sun instead of silky blond locks that gave off light.

TURTLE EGGS

By the time we were back in Kuching, I was undergoing puberty, and this was deeply uncomfortable. My body was morphing in unpleasant ways, sprouting large breasts and giving me a circular, soft shape. I felt about three times the size of most Malaysian women and girls. Relatives commented on how "big" I was. I grew sullen. Being back "home," I felt more alien than ever before.

We spent those weeks consuming noodle dishes, seafood wok-fried in lemongrass and shallots, crispy greens tinged with belacan—the blend of spices, garlic, and galangal making us unusually gassy. Still, I found it thoroughly delectable. Turtle egg soup, on the other hand...I cannot bear to eat unscrambled chicken eggs, let alone these translucent, gooey, soft eggs offered to me by my aunt and uncle. But it was a delicacy, and I was their grateful guest who would never dare decline such hospitality out of fear of perceived rudeness. I asked for a glass of

Coke and proceeded to heave down the eggs in between gulps of pop, determined to prove my gratitude for such a delicacy. After the fourth, I asked for more to drink. My uncle's wife exclaimed: "Oh, I guess you like it! Would you like more eggs?" I gracefully declined, intoning that I was so full and thank you so very much. But perhaps I possessed acting skills par excellence and had performed genuine delight too realistically because my aunty, a slim and sweet woman, insisted on refilling my bowl.

"No, no, I can't. It's too much to ask for, save some for yourselves," I said.

"It's our pleasure," she replied. "You don't visit so often."

I finally got out of it by asking for dessert.

I suddenly longed for the familiarity of those processed foods in Canada, the other home. My taste buds had crossed over. While there were still Malaysian dishes I relished, the thought of mac 'n' cheese now seemed comforting. My allegiances were mixed.

To this day, I have a texture/taste memory of the squishy rounds and the sulfurous tang of yolk lodged in my mind. Just thinking of it makes me want to retch.

HUNGER

When we returned to Canada, I soon began my first year in high school. Unsure of my own changing body, of my shifting allegiances to the motherland, and the uncertainties about belonging. I sought a harbour for my insecurities, to find my own tribe.

Within months, I fell into a no man's land. An awkward teenager becoming a woman, part nerd and part non-Canadian.

I couldn't reside comfortably in the homeland.

I wasn't entirely accepted in the chosen land.

I was alien inside my own skin, estranged from the mutating curves of my body.

There was no internal home to return to.

Exercise became my religion. Measuring out my food and counting calories. I started running every day (and I hate running). On bad weather days, I blasted music in the basement and did a dance workout. After three months, my period stopped. At fifteen, I weighed, depending on the hour (I weighed myself several times a day), seventy-eight pounds with my clothes on. My stomach rebelled, churning constantly as if I had eaten something bad. I had figured that my earlier diet of dairy and junk food had contributed to my curves, so I obsessed about fruits and greens, another cellular conversion that actually did alter my digestive system forever.

During my high school years, my parents scrutinized my marks as judiciously as I had counted calories. While I got A's in almost everything, my mom (an accountant) and dad (an engineer) were concerned about my B- in math. To their dismay, I was the outlier, the only kid in the family unable to achieve an A in math.

Monitoring. Managing. Everything was a form of regulation—being the perfect student, being an obedient daughter. Squished and re-formed into something like cheese slices in plastic wrap. Easy to see and ingest. My childhood years were about enduring the scrutiny of my parents while also trying to be embraced and accepted by Canadian society at large.

My family does not talk about the year I weighed seventy-eight pounds. Once in my thirties, we did casually chat about my focus on running and that I got thin. But we stopped—lest we veer into unknown territory, an empire of sadness, insecurity, and shifting identities. The body is a temple of history. These days, I get cramps whenever I don't eat enough vegetables or fruit. My body craves fibre in large quantities due to my insane weight-loss regime in my teen years. My digestive system was altered, it's out of sorts. Steeped in pain, my body knows its past.

CHEESE

I have two countries and one body. Milk, butter, and cottage cheese are regulars in my fridge. And about twice a year, I hanker for K.D. Ice cream is a staple in hot months. In my mid-twenties, I studied in France to improve my French skills and developed a taste for soft cheeses, especially brie, the gateway cheese that led me to the delights of Reblochon, buffalo mozzarella, and mild Gouda. Cheese opened a whole other world of possibilities. My other staples are rice and savoury stir-fries.

When did my blood metamorphize?

When did the borders of my vessels turn porous?

When did I become a foreign body?

The curries and chili sauces that raced through my veins have transformed into milk,

the rice-noodle arteries supplanted by bucatini,

my chili crab heart replaced by a rib-eye steak.

BUTTER

In Malaysia, Danish butter cookies in a royal blue tin were prized as a kind of European token. If you could afford them or hand them out during holiday periods, it meant things were going well. A reassuring sign. In Germany, where I live now, I discovered a delightful phrase, alles in butter!—which means that everything is fine. Butter stands for good.

I am the embodiment of all the multitudes of experiences I've digested.

I haven't been back to Malaysia since.

I do not fit in there. It's too late.

The milk has solidified.

The cream is set.

All is in butter.

MAHTA RIAZI

Ligaments

We are ligaments, all that connects. When they tell me about the breast, they say: picture a constellation, chain-link fences. A line of moon-faced children holding hands. That's what I see on the diagram that the oncologist spins her screen all the way around to show me. Globules of fat and oblong ducts separated by rivers of lymph nodes and walls of fibrous tissue.

"Everything is connected in the breast," Dr. Yassa says, her eyes puffy and purple with tired bags. She rubs them, taking off her glasses, her voice calm and sure like someone explaining the rotation of planets to a curious child. This is just the way things are. Mercury is hot. Venus has no moons.

"We can't just remove the tumour," she says, "we must remove the whole breast, just to be sure. It's the safest thing to do."

A week earlier, on a cold grocery walk home, my fingers holding together a broken and bursting maxi bag, half a joint between my fingers, and the phone clamped between my head and my shoulder, a doctor had told me that cancer cells had been found in my biopsy report. The little lump that I had been told the previous summer was nothing to worry about had become something to worry about.

I had walked slowly to my east Plateau apartment and sat for hours on the wobbly chair in my kitchen, staring at the small painted plates of Qajar-era women that hung on my wall. Their expressions were mysteriously neutral under the monobrow that shadowed their eyes. They were petite, flat-chested. In my mind, I peeled my body off like a mango, sat in my skeleton and watched the fear figure eight around my rib cage.

My childhood and teen years coincided with a time in Hollywood in which cancer movies were having a moment; all of those heart-wrenching stories that eventually culminated in heartwarming tales that brought families closer together. This is what life had made of my expectations. Love's prevalence. The inevitability of family. But the months that followed my diagnosis were absent of silver linings. Guilt and grief met in the back of a bar and destroyed each other, held nothing back. Breast cancer materialized, like bubbles of oil to the surface, deep-seated and uncomfortable conversations around gender presentation and sexuality that had been carefully and comfortably avoided in previous years in my family. I felt responsible—as if I had manifested the cleaving off of my most feminine asset.

"God takes from you what you are not grateful for," my mother used to tell me. She mourned and mourned my gone womanhood, picturing her plump and healthy lineage curved against the ghost of a chest.

When the winter at last showed the first signs of melting away, the long and jagged scar across my chest a satisfying shade of pink, my mother clasped, with all her might, at a spidery thread of hope, and refused to let go. She presented my family with a solution to our heartbreak.

"I think it's time for a visit home."

My sister and I were lucky enough to spend many summers of our childhood in Tehran, surrounded by family, watching our parents transform in the confidence and comfort of being in a home they knew.

My mother laughing with her sisters. My father gifting a yellow dress to his niece. We saw these moments. We understood that distance was a feeling.

My parents had left the country in 1989 when my father was granted a student bursary to study molecular biology in Edmonton. He was to return to Iran, work, raise his family. We were never supposed to stay. But as Iran was plunged deeper into economic difficulty, following decades of stifling Western sanctions, we stayed. We moved to Toronto, settled into a Regent Park apartment, became Iranian Canadians. Collecting scratch-off calling cards in a corner of the kitchen table. Driving to Niagara Falls on long weekends. Waiting for summers in Iran.

In the early years, when we'd arrive at the airport in Tehran, we'd be treated like celebrities. My mother's huge family would stand behind the glass at Mehrabad International Airport with bouquets of flowers in their hands, eyes glistening, jumping with excitement. When I was small enough to be carried, I remember being passed from arm to arm, pinched and smothered in a blur of kisses. I remember picturing myself crowd-surfing like in movies I'd seen, all that love carrying me to the warm, gasoline-scented air outside.

Our family's arrival was an opportunity and excuse for everyone to gather. Old fights would be resolved or be pushed to autumn. Spontaneous road trips to the Caspian would be arranged. Not a day would pass that we weren't invited to someone's home. I'd spend the days following my grandmother, a devout Ashtyani woman, as she fed the pale-chested pigeons on the balcony. I'd play gorgam be hava with my cousins in the cracked and mouldy waterless pool in my aunt's yard, where in each cracked corner, small yellow flowers sprouted among bunches of weeds.

We silenced our grief with these memories on the plane ride over.

Do you remember Amoo Ismail always snoring in the back room? May God grant mercy to his soul.

Remember the year Moha and I painted all the tiles on the balcony? And how we wept when the rain washed it all off?

Remember all the laughter?

Everyone stuffed together in red-carpeted rooms?

We told story after story on the plane until our excitement bubbled off the wings and into the night's blinking sky. All our hope, like eggs in a Tehran-shaped basket. "Ay vatan," Baba said from his seat, his hand beating against his chest. Oh, homeland. We were going back to Iran and surely it would wash all the salt from our wounds, all the mud from our hair. It was Norouz. A new day, a new beginning. Enough, enough with the loneliness and sorrow and rooms holding all the pain of the past six months. We would find our way back to one another. This is what life had made of our expectations: home is what heals us.

Inshallah.

Some kinds of losses are simple. Black and white. They either shatter your heart into pieces small enough to slide between teeth—or they don't.

Losing a body part. Losing a country. Those are the complicated kinds of loss.

A few days before my left breast was sliced like a pear off my terrified body, my dear friend Rou, a quiet and thoughtful photographer, showed up with a camera and a notebook to my third-floor apartment. She took photos of my body, before it became mismatched. Me lying on my bed. Me looking in the mirror. Hands by my side. Hands folded across my chest. "Don't smile," she kept reminding me, "look natural."

Before she took the photos, she had asked if it would be okay to pose some questions. We sat on square brown chairs, our faces lost in the fog of steam rising from our teacups. My chair made a clicking sound each time I moved, the back screw loose. Rou wondered:

What thoughts were going through my head with the mastectomy approaching?

How did I anticipate saying goodbye to this body part?

What was my relationship with my breasts?

I was unsure how to answer. "It's complicated," I had said. "They hold so much…discomfort." They've been punched and squeezed and poked at without my permission. They've connected me to a femininity I resented yet felt intimately obligated to.

In truth, there is little to say of occupancy, of ownership. Sometimes hidden, sometimes not. But *never guarded, never protected, never safe.* Even with all that padding.

On that day, the surgery was less than forty-eight hours away. "There's not enough time," I had told Rou. There was not enough time, and I was unsure what a body needed. My body, with its rivers and valleys and *patience.* My untimely remorse that showed up anyway, head hanging.

More than anything, I was sorry. I apologized to my body, begging for its forgiveness. *God takes from you what you are not grateful for.* Rou listened to my pleas and sobs, waiting patiently, her hand on my arm.

She said, "Tell me when you're ready."

"My body is a place," writes poet M. Soledad Caballero. "Part of something beyond bone and rage."

A few months after our plane landed in Tehran that mid-March night, the heartbeat of a young Kurdish woman would be silenced. The straw would land. The camel would collapse. The bloodied hands of tyrants from every direction would scramble to beat the drums of their own interests. Sons and daughters, and all between and beyond, would swarm the streets chest-first, growing like mitosis, multiplying by the day. It would come as no surprise after decades of patience thinned from grief and resentment. Of the choke of inflation and theft and greed.

Nothing had happened yet. But we could feel it, from the night we arrived. The tired, aching body of a city we arrogantly thought we still knew. Acres of air in front of us, dense.

Tehran had changed. Of course, Tehran had changed. It had been six years. Half-built buildings lay open like surgical patients in the shadow of large cranes. Baba pointed at the new high-rises in disbelief. "Tehran has changed." He stated the obvious.

In the weeks that followed, I reached for the familiar, my finger poised on the window, looking for Waldo, for Kolah Ghermezi. Stray cats with patches of missing fur hiding under cars. The trees jutting out in the middle of streets. That old, abandoned Qajar-era house with dogs barking violently inside its prison of yellow brick walls.

Along the highway, my eyes would cling to the tops of trees and the illumination of billboards. Qasem Soleimani with a halo, thick wings sprouting from his broad shoulders. Qasem Soleimani in the arms of the Prophet, his face invisible behind a bright white light. In a few short months, many of these, including the one where Soleimani's head rests pensively in the crutch of his own curled palm, would be torched in the early hours of the morning, smoke blurring and breaking the sun's arrival.

The last time I had been to Iran had been six years before, when I was twenty, long-haired, and singing for a crowd at my cousin's wedding. I was a good daughter. I was not a mismatched body. There is a photo of me wearing a long, pastel dress at the wedding, a photo my mother often returns to, brimming with longing. She strokes the sides of my pixelated face. She says, "The evil eye was on our family that night."

It is my mother's way of imprisoning a drop of reality. Of possessing it. Making sure it doesn't get away. This is what life had made of my mother's expectations: loss, loss, loss. A new country overnight. The disappearance of neighbours. Lonely winters. The evil eye. She's learned to hold on to the body like an anchor. She asks it questions. She begs it to remind her of everything she once possessed.

She is nostalgic, she cannot help it.

Neither can I.

"Tenses," Audre Lorde says, "are a way of ordering the chaos around time." We place ourselves in one moment, then another. We move forward and back. We remember what used to be. We trace the path of what could. The body, then, is perhaps a way of ordering the chaos around grief. We see the scars. We remember what used to be. We trace the path of what could.

We understand distance as a feeling.

I haven't yet asked to look at the pictures Rou took of my premastectomy body. I have not wanted to look back, afraid of what I'd see. I can sometimes believe I am brand new now, that I am no longer all I am attached to. That I can tell myself new stories.

That summer did not disappear the cratered distances within my family. But it did allow us to stand in the dark. There, where there is only the body. Where one learns how far forgiveness can stretch, how it holds infinite shapes.

How it becomes connective tissue.

AYESHA HABIB

What Remains
of Home

I've been thinking about pigeons lately. No matter how far you take one from its birthplace, it will find its way back home. It's one of the many mysteries of nature, an instinctual, primal urge in their souls. A pigeon has only one home; it knows where it belongs.

Sometimes I wonder if humans were designed with that same conviction, that same absoluteness of home. But somewhere along the way, in the eons of evolution and migration, we've forgotten, and in our confusion we ache for a primal sort of belonging. I wonder if it's this forgotten instinct in my blood that pulls me back to my childhood home in the moments when I feel the most home-less: when my melancholy was born, when my innocence rotted into bitterness, when my father died.

I was born in Nairobi, Kenya, as a third-generation Indian Ismaili. My childhood was rust-red roads and exhaust fumes. It was torrential rainfalls that left as quickly as they arrived and constant power outages. It was searching for fairies in our garden and watching the birds build nests in the trees outside my window. It was monkeys that once got into our kitchen and stole all of our fruit, and lizards that scurried up walls and sometimes dropped to the ground or on top of our heads. It was Swahili and English and Gujarati and Kutchi. It was fresh chapati off the stove and meat on charcoal barbecues and samosas and biryani and ugali and tandoori. It was jamatkhana (mosque) every Friday evening and Ma and Bapa's (my father's parents) house every Sunday morning.

It was innocence and pure belonging.

I was nine when my father's work as a banker took us to Dubai. There, I saw my mother cry for the first time, homesick for the world she had known all her life. My own melancholy first stirred inside me during this time. I was growing, but not proportionally or gracefully. I was lanky limbs and buck teeth and inflamed acne and a dark, fuzzy moustache. My peers, who came from all around the world, seemed crueller than the friends I left behind. I was teased for many things: my quietness, my glasses, my frizzy hair, my hairy legs.

At barely eleven, I was becoming bitter, an outcast. I wrapped myself in the only good memories I had, which were all in Kenya. Even though I was still a child, I romanticized the idyllic haze of childhood. I constantly daydreamed of my return. In my head, everything I hated about myself would go away once I was back home. My skin would become smooth, my hair sleek, my secret beauty would finally, *finally* arrive. I would be graceful and confident and loved by all.

A year later, over summer vacation, we visited Kenya—my father, mother, brother, and me. I returned heavier in my heart than when I left, but I was happy, nonetheless. We returned to all the familiar places, and even though it hadn't been very long since we'd left, I adored on every space like it had been a century. We visited the food court in the mall, where we once owned an Indian-Kenyan fusion outlet and that now had new owners. They retained the old menu, but the food tasted blander, like cut corners and cheap ingredients. Then, at my request, we went to the giraffe centre, where we could feed rescued giraffes by hand.

My love for animals had only grown since leaving Kenya, and, in returning, I felt, more than ever, an almost spiritual connection to all the creatures of this land. I often daydreamed of acquiring the ability to speak to animals, and secretly believed that this power would one day present itself and confirm, with a spiritual sense of absoluteness, that I belonged to this world. I tried, telepathically, to urge the giraffe to understand me, to see in me a sense of kinship and love. Instead, I only received a long slimy tongue, coiling around the treats in my hand.

We visited our old home with permission from the new owners, an elderly English couple. It was smaller than I remembered. It smelled different, though I could not quite place how. I walked through familiar rooms filled with unfamiliar furniture. Is there a word for that surreal feeling of existing in a space that is both home and unknown? Still, my return trip only solidified my conviction that Kenya was my true home, that any other place I lived was only temporary.

It's been fifteen years since we left. I haven't been back since.

I was twelve when my father uprooted us again and took us to Canada. This time, to start the gruelling process of permanent residency, then citizenship. We settled in a North Vancouver neighbourhood, becoming one of the only non-white families on the block. It's here that I would see my father cry for the first time. It's here where I would witness my family's downfall.

There's a specific sadness in watching your parents awkwardly navigate new homes, new social situations, new ways of talking and being. Aside from a few relatives in Canada who they could never truly connect to, they were friendless. My father left his job to start his own financial advice business, and his days of tailored suits and client dinners were replaced with shabby T-shirts and a tiny home office. My mother, already deeply misunderstood by the friends and family in her life, was driven further into internal solitude. Back home, they were social butterflies, always out, always readying for guests. In Canada, they spent most of their nights in front of the TV. But they had each other.

We didn't know how to move in this new country; we were graceless. And, for the first time, we were faced with our otherness. It hinted itself in small ways. A rude note stuck in my father's windshield wiper. A dirty look from the neighbour. And once, at a small-town restaurant during a summer road trip, we were seated outside, in a back alley next to the dumpster.

There was a coldness here beyond the new climate. My own advantage during this time was being young and malleable. I was determined not to be seen as the outcast I was in Dubai. Here, I understood quickly that my foreignness made me different, so I ascribed to whiteness like it was godliness. I secretly bought a razor so I could shave my arms, I changed the cadences and inflections of my voice to mimic the girls in my class, I pretended to like the same food they did—even when it was tasteless or overwrought with processed cheese. But I knew I was a fraud. Every step I took into that world felt like I was wearing shoes on the wrong feet. My melancholy swallowed me whole.

I thought often of home. I had intrinsically tangled my Kenyan birthplace with my identity. It continued to be the space I'd return to in my daydreams, when the bitter cold of my new home became unbearable.

It wasn't until I reached university that I began to unlearn the pressure to be white. During my first few days at the dorm, I met a boy from Mombasa, on the coast of Kenya. But I found I had nothing substantial to say to him. It had been ten years since I had moved away. I only knew the country through a child's eyes, through fragmented memories. I had no claim to belong there.

My daydreams of home were becoming undone thread by thread.

I began, instead, to search for belonging in my Indian identity—an identity I had never quite felt comfortable wearing. Until then, I had always considered myself Kenyan with Indian heritage. My parents and grandparents were born in Kenya; it was my great-grandparents who emigrated from Gujarat. I had never lived in India, I did not speak any Indian languages, and I knew nothing of its history.

I enrolled in a class on Indian contemporary literature where I read Arundhati Roy and Vikram Seth. I watched Indian cinema—important films about partition, Hindu nationalism, police corruption, caste systems. I looked into the history of my people, the Ismailis, to trace their communities stemming from Persia to Gujarat to East Africa and around the world. Yet still, I felt like a fraud whenever I mispronounced a word like desi or simply didn't know what a lehenga was.

I felt perpetually unwanted by all different factions of me. I belonged only to memories.

It was around this time when, as part of a semester abroad, I spent three months living in Uganda. I had never been closer to home. It was barely an hour's flight away, but I could not face the feeling of being a stranger in the place I was born, as I feared would happen. I was also beginning to reconsider my space in this specific section of the world. In Kampala, where Asians were once violently expelled from the country to allow more opportunities for native Africans, I began to research the history of Indian presence in Africa. I started to understand the role of Indian diasporic communities in East Africa with much more nuance than I ever did before. I learned how Indian communities were afforded, by the British, economic privileges over Africans, which granted them social power and wealth still experienced today. I could no longer romanticize my childhood without facing the historical privileges of my community. If I was ever to return to Kenya, I wanted to be ready: I needed to untether my emotional (sometimes I feared they were colonial) notions of my home country from the reality of its complex history.

It was always understood in my family that we would do another return trip to Kenya, most likely once I had graduated university. But in the end, Canada's coldness had the last laugh in the cackle of an over-burdened healthcare system. During my last semester, my father fell ill. But it would take six months for him to get a cancer diagnosis that could trigger treatment. In the sizable gaps between specialist appointments and follow-ups, the brain tumour grew, expanding its monster-like ten-tacles outward, enmeshing itself so furiously into his brain matter that it would be impossible to cut it out cleanly. He died four months after the official diagnosis.

Recently, my mother told me she doesn't think she could ever return to Kenya. The memories of the life they lived there, she and my dad, are too painful to come back to.

Home is no longer quite what it used to be. It is an imperfect mem-ory of childhood, saturated in rosy colours of nostalgia. Homesickness is an ache to return to childlike innocence, to a time before my melan-choly, a time before coldness.

I take comfort in the concept of imagined homelands written about by Salman Rushdie. Writing specifically about Indian authors living in England, Rushdie says that there's an inevitable sense of loss when looking back to the homeland. For these writers, who try to return to India with words, they can only replicate a fragmented version, based on imperfect, nostalgic memory. These fictionalized versions of home are the imaginary homelands, and it is here where Rushdie finds value. In the *London Review of Books*, he wrote: "The shards of memory acquired greater status, greater resonance, because they were *remains*; fragmentation made trivial things seem like symbols, and the mundane acquired numinous qualities."

The imagined homeland I return to in my head is a specific, fragmented version of the home I knew until I was nine years old. It is exaggerated and romantic, and the only place I've ever felt I belonged. Yet I do have hope, stemming from the abundance of this memory, that when I do return, I will know I belong.

KRISTA EIDE

Land Between Lake and Sea

My vertigo is a seasickness—not a spinning sensation, but a voyage across the roiling Atlantic. I can walk a straight line, but my vision lists—left-right, left-right—from the moment I wake until sleep. It's been three months, and no one can explain it, nothing can be done for it. It'll just go away, the doctors say, but I'm worried I'll be like this for the rest of my life—my eyes, brain, and inner ears colluding to upset the world.

In January, my sister and I surprised our dad with a seventieth birthday gift—a father-daughter trip to Norway, to the village his father emigrated from as a young man in 1921. We've made fall plans to connect with distant cousins and explore the region. I never knew my grandfather—he died suddenly in 1959, when Dad was thirteen. Dad choked up when he opened the card, but still managed to quip: "If I'm still around by then." He's been dying of something or another for my entire life.

I'd hoped to be well by the time we left for Norway, but now it's September and my computer screen blurs and bobs. Two days before our flight, I curl around myself on my office floor and call my sister, sobbing. "I can't go," I tell her.

She's stern: "If I can, you can." She's recently developed a crippling fear of flying.

In the car to YVR, everything tilts and tilts. My father seems nervous. He looks thinner than usual, more tired. Is it just his aging, or is something actually wrong with him? My sister rubs circles into her temples. Afternoon sun floods the back seat. "It's too nice here to leave," Dad says. My sister and I silently agree. We feel safe here, our bodies tethered by gravity to this land.

On the red-eye to London Heathrow, my sister drowns her sleeping pills in white wine and passes out mid-dinner. For nine long hours, my father and I toss and turn against each other under our thin airline blankets.

Oslo is a gorgeous harbourside city whose edges recede into forests and mountains, not unlike Vancouver. Although the Oslo I experience is filtered through my tick-tocking vision and my unease is heightened by jet lag. The massive ninth-century vessels at the Viking Ship Museum conjure heaving bodies pulling oars in stormy seas. In Frogner Park, Gustav Vigeland's outdoor granite sculpture, *The Monolith*, is a tower of desperate, naked humans scrambling over one another to reach the sky. At every café the coffee is black rocket fuel that sets my hands trembling.

At the Munch Museum, we watch a short film about Edvard Munch. Losing his mother and sister as a child set the tone for his life and work. He was anxious, depressed, agoraphobic, obsessed with illness and death. In the gallery, I absorb the churning waters and agitated skies of *Angst* and think about dark Nordic winters. If only nineteenth-century Norwegians had had SSRIs. Although, I can't be smug, with my half-Scandinavian genes, my decades lived in the grey light and peevish drizzle of coastal British Columbia. Outside the museum is a large golden frame and we each take a turn standing inside it, slapping our cheeks and making our mouths into silent Os—Instagram-ready versions of *The Scream*.

Four days in Oslo and our circadian rhythms are still out of sync. We three find each other at odd hours in our Airbnb's kitchen—my father frail in his rumpled sleep clothes, my sister with dark circles under her eyes. We consult maps, find where to collect our rental car, plan our road trip to the ancestral village. "My shoulder," Dad says. He windmills his left arm in the dim light. "It's probably angina."

My sister gives me a look. "You probably slept on it weird," she tells him.

My grandfather's hometown in the western fjordlands is a five-hour drive from Oslo, but it's missing from our *Lonely Planet* guide. We're dazzled by each landscape we move through—desolate tundra that drops into a valley of prematurely bronze birches, shorefront cottages with electric-green sod roofs. Each body of water is so still, I can't tell if it's salt or fresh. Yet, as we approach our destination, my anxiety surges. Throat tightens, vision blurs. "You're fine," Dad says. Then he too starts to feel it—a dizziness that surfaces as he drives. He opens the window.

One Sunday afternoon two years ago, lightning shot through my spinal column, my heart jolted, and my scalp went numb. And then again, a few days later. And then every day. After a year, the panic attacks mostly subsided, but left their memory hidden in my body like a dormant virus. Now I suspect this vertigo is just anxiety in another form, yet I still think the worst—a fatal brain tumour squeezing my inner ear, tilting the earth from its axis. Of course, this thought is also suspect.

The highway terminates at a ferry dock and we park behind a lone vehicle. The small vessel approaches, framed in blue layers—sea, mountain, sky. This fjord could be Howe Sound, this berth a Gulf Island landing. Only the mountains are different—not the jagged, volcanic spine I'm used to, but peaks with smooth edges, landforms mellowed by a longer geological lifetime. Then, just when the setting starts to feel familiar, it disorients. On the other shore of the fjord, we disembark and drive straight into a tunnel. The gears struggle, the car slows. It takes us a long minute to understand that, in this dark tube, we are climbing.

We reach our rental by late afternoon, a cornflower-blue cottage on the edge of a lake. Everything is quiet and serene, yet the whitewashed walls close in. I swallow an Ativan and step onto the deck. Across the lake, fine waterfalls drizzle down the mountainside, so steady they appear frozen. The tinkling of brass bells—goats grazing in the distant hills. The twilight air is damp. Calm floods my veins. Later, I burrow under a heavy duvet and drift into a dreamless sleep.

In the morning, our Norwegian cousin Odd-Kore arrives at our cottage to guide us to Sandane, the nearby village where he and his family live in my grandfather's childhood home. He is a round-faced dairy farmer who speaks softly in hesitant English. We follow his car ten kilometres down the highway to a rural road, then pull up to a small white farmhouse. Beyond it, rolling fields are dotted with cows and framed by distant mountains. This place was passed down from his grandfather— my grandfather's oldest brother. We are astonished to see that the property and house, even the mountain view, are nearly identical to the Fraser Valley hobby farm where Dad was raised in the house built by his father.

Our cousin takes us to the village churchyard, and we find our last name, rare in Canada, on dozens of gravestones. In Norwegian, our name means isthmus, or, more precisely, "the land between lake and sea," which is where this town lies—between the northwestern shore of Breimsvatnet Lake, where we're staying, and the fingertip of Gloppen- fjorden. Some part of us belongs to this sliver of land, has belonged here a long time. The idea is both comforting and confining.

After a few days in the village, stillness settles into my body. Then my vertigo picks up again, like a maelstrom gathering force.

Odd-Kore's older sister arrives from a nearby town, curious to meet us. When she sees my father, she begins to cry. He looks just like a favou- rite cousin who's recently died, she explains through tears. Dad doesn't know what to do with this. "Ja, ja," he says, nodding. "Ja, ja." Throat catching, eyes watering—as though he's the ghost of that cousin, as though he's a man whose father never left this country.

"Let's hit the road," Dad says. Back home, he's an amateur historian known to take new friends on eight-hour driving tours around B.C.— no charge, just for pleasure. But in Norway, his usual sociable self is tamped down. Before our visit with our cousins is through, he's eager to say goodbye to these living links to his father. Dad was a boy who lost his father at age thirteen, his mother at seventeen.

(I nearly lost Dad when I was fourteen, a fact I've half-submerged in my memory's depths. His months-long illness, the guilt-stained relief each time I exited the hospital into the soft spring light, my mind turning to lunch or music or books—anything.)

The spoken Norwegian contains a word that's an ingressive sound— a quick, inhaled "ha!" It's an exclamation of incredulity, or an affirmation that one is listening, as English speakers might insert "wow" or "uh-huh" as someone tells a story. Sometimes the word is soft, barely audible, sometimes it is startling, like a drowning person breaking the surface to gasp for oxygen. I jump when our Norwegian cousins unconsciously use it as they speak English. This sharp inhale becomes a family joke— my father's, my sister's, and mine. Although, in the privacy of our rental cottage, we use it the way we understand it—to scare each other.

I'd always thought Dad was just being pessimistic when he'd say, "I'm dying." I thought it was mortal dread from his parents' deaths, or residual trauma from his real illness years ago. *Hypochondria*, our mother taught us young. No one said anxiety disorder in the eighties. Nobody understood panic attacks. Only recently did I realize my father might actually feel those pains—the lung squeezes, the lightning strikes. I understand now because I've arrived at the emergency room, believing I was near death, and been completely wrong.

Before my grandfather boarded a ship to Canada, my great-grandmother pointed out a young pine on the family property and told her son that was his tree. My grandfather embraced the tree and swore to his mother he'd return to measure his absence with his arms. As we say our goodbyes, Odd-Kore tells us this story and describes the tree. On the road back, we find it standing tall, the only pine among the remains of its felled neighbours. My grandfather never returned home, never again saw his parents and siblings, his country. Ninety-five years later, his son and granddaughters complete his journey. Dad wraps his arms around its trunk while I take photos. My father's eyes are wet, but his face won't tell me anything else.

We drive south to Bergen, where Dad's mood lifts as we stroll the harbour and ride the funicular up the mountainside. My vertigo must be subsiding because I keep asking myself, *Do I feel it, do I feel it?* like a teenager after her first beer.

We've planned to visit other Scandinavian highlights, so we fly to Copenhagen, where the land is flat and sun shimmers across the canals. September rushes toward October. In Stockholm, rain falls in fat, cold drops. The vertigo has finally left my body.

On the final day of our trip, we're walking to the Stockholm metro to go sightseeing when Dad stops, clutches his chest, says he feels weird. "It's a panic attack," I tell him. "Breathe." My sister and I each take an arm and walk our father back to the Airbnb, where I bring him Ativan and chamomile tea. I turn on Swedish television and we sink into the sofa in a strange family's home. I'm still worried something worse than anxiety is wrong with Dad. Then I realize he must be exhausted from the trip, from being confronted with the past, from keeping up with his daughters. Maybe homesickness has infected his body like a cold.

The next morning, we head to the airport to trace our route home to Vancouver. When the Fraser River and jagged Coast Range come into view, and we're minutes from landing, all three of us lean toward the tiny airplane window and anticipate the ground.

ALEXANDRA C. YEBOAH

The Motherland Knows My Name

a poetic essay

1.   arrival: i make my way through the pulsing market in accra, ghana, unbound in sweat, exhilaration, and childlike hope. i exist within this space of time as the protagonist in a coming-of-age novel; a debut artist on stage for the first time. i am a timorous lamb: my ghanaian-born father and aunt the shepherds entrusted to lead me through the colossal throng of shuffling bodies that occupy the expansive retail area. vendor booths line the congested streets inches from midday traffic, and proposition tourists with an array of enticing goods: bananas, plantain, yams, mangos, rice, fish, and bread. as i pass through the market, hawkers left and right extend prying, frenzied hands toward me, their staccato haggling with single-minded buyers deepening with proximity.

when i finally meet my kin in the middle, the restless crowd parts like the red sea and enfolds me like a wayward child.

a. to embrace: nothing can adequately describe what it's like to open yourself up to a place you had always felt and *believed* in, but had never been close enough to experience.

b. indebtedness: the *motherland* has permitted me entrance into her tantalizing, sacred abode.

2.   invitation: when someone wants to share a meal with you the opening line is "you're invited."

a.   *body parts talking:* at uncle s's unadorned, no-frills dinner table, i sit with my extended relatives: uncle s, aunt j, and three of my revered cousins. mealtime: my roused, umber *eyes* drink in the deep-fried plantains, the red stew, the *waakye*, and the candied yams.

duly convinced of the calibre of the meal in front of me, my *stomach* mutters something along the lines of: "*i'm ready, feed me!*" my *eyes* politely request that my stomach wait, but not before offering a bit of assurance, *food is coming your way, don't you worry…*

my eyes observe with surprise and secret glee as all seated at the table dig into their meals without forks or spoons. my *stomach* advises my *hands* to be assertive, and go for what the collective digestive unit requires. therefore my usually modest, dutiful *hands* become the intrepid eating tools i freely employ to partake in this jubilant feast.

my *frontal lobe* learns that it is not improper to eat with your hands: it is customary here.

3. double-dutch

a.   first *sound waves:* the melodious giggles in the near distance
play tug-of-war and rope me closer into the designated point of
interest.

    b.   visual confirmation: i see a group of preteen girls skipping rope
        near some mud houses in kumasi, ghana. their unrestrained joy
        is contagious. watching their lithe bodies bounce in time to
        ropes that slap the reddened soil, frees something wildly
        exhilarating in me.

        c. triggering release: the voice of my childlike self demands to
        jump in. i heed to her will, just as the tallest girl on the right
        sporting shiny black braids and dimpled cheeks looks in my
        direction. i ask if i can have a turn. she nods.

        when i trip the first time, laughter punctures the air. curious
        adults form a half-circle around me as i permit myself to
        indulge further. choosing to participate in this childhood game,
        i take hold of a moment that belongs to me only; it grants me
        ample opportunity to soar beyond my self-constrained limits.

4. are you listening?

problem: i think the waiter at the restaurant wants to take my order,
but he is talking twi. he doesn't know yet that i can only converse in
english.

makeshift solution: i think it best not to interrupt his train of thought,
so i remain quietly seated, in the effort to appear attentive. a mona lisa

half-smile squirms like a callow pupa onto my face.

when i hear: "..............*wo ho te se*............"
i gush out: "*eh ye!*" (the only twi i know)

the final answer: rather than reply, the waiter gives me a funny
look. my cousin and her boyfriend watch the exchange, amused.

confusion: my cousin offers an explanation: "the waiter
wonders why you didn't answer earlier.

he doesn't understand that you don't speak the language...he
thought you were ignoring him all this time."

oh.

5. stop requested: there is no siri voice to let you know of your
upcoming stop on the *tro tro*. you just have to know when to get off.

6. this is before:

a.   *the first time* i visited the motherland i played with stray kittens
in uncle p's compound in dormaa.

i sat on the front steps and watched as my favourite kitty
wedged herself between the others, as if she had every right to
be there. she had spunk, chutzpah (lots of it); she wasn't the
type to wait around to be invited.

enamoured, i asserted my six-year-old presence by crouching
down behind the mixed kitten like a praying mantis and

lunging at her. when she retreated, i clawed at her scrawny tail to reel her back in.

uncle p clapped in the background, as if watching an oscar-worthy performance. "you wish to take the little cats home?" he says. *cats, plural.*

no, just one. my heart leapt in my throat at the mere possibility. i turn to my dad, questioning, hopeful.

"how? they won't allow us to take pets on the plane" was my dad's calculated response.

b. *the first time* i saw a desperate chicken scramble for its life. right before its steadfast pursuer put it out of its misery. the prospective poultry dish flailed around the block with its skewed head; a final protest. when the guttural strangling sounds started, my insides spun around like a perpetual wash cycle. the faithfully stagnant yet panicked observer i was, i stood my ground while the appointed butcher carried on in theatrical fluidity.

what is left behind: 1. a headless chicken 2. an unruly witness: also known as me

my plate at dinner that evening (chicken and jollof rice) goes cold.

c. *the first time* featured an initial meeting with my paternal grandmother, a stalwart woman in her late nineties. as i perched on my father's mother's lap, her crumpled hands latched themselves to me, sealing me to her. she held me close enough for my swollen pigtails to obscure the left side of her face. i sat in place for what felt like hours; uncertain, and distrustful of this strange, imposing figure. i thought about climbing down and running away.

in the family album, the matriarch i barely knew presented a closed, toothless smile, with dancing eyes. i wore a frumpish pout.

the first time was also the last time.

d. *the first time* i saw my aunty p wrap my one-year-old sister on her back. she placed the cerulean-blue kente around my sister's small body and looped her closer, cocooning her in safety and rising promise.

7. this is after: *the second time* i travel to ghana i am much older: i'm twenty-two and idealistic, having just landed my first career job a mere two months after graduating.

i leave this same cushy office job a year and a half later, eager to venture
off the western front and explore new possibilities.

8. the science of fufu:

when i come back from my stroll in aburi gardens that day, i find auntie j mixing a white doughy flour mix with what looks to be a grotesquely enlarged baseball bat. she pounds the sticky-like substance into a dull brown earthenware bowl.

"do you want to try?" aunty j says when she notices me watching. i step forward: timid, unsure.

aunty j hands me the wooden pestle: my delicate hands fumble with its weight. within minutes my arms begin to tingle from the unfamiliar, repetitive motion. i hand the pestle back over to auntie j, weary and apologetic. she tosses me an aloof smile, then powers on as if she had never stopped.

9. disservice: when one of my father's friends greets me during my visit to his part of the country,

i instinctively wave my left hand.

"do. not. *ever* raise you left hand *anywhere* in africa," he says to me.

i am *mortified* = must regain my dignity.

"it's your," i say.

10. first-class orphans: the term my cousin's boyfriend calls a group of residents from a city orphanage because the director refused to accept my *lightly used* clothing donations. my attempt at charity had been politely tossed back in my face.

11. displacement

"one day I'm going to get all of *you people* off our land, i swear to god," an entitled stranger says to me in passing at a community centre in brampton.

i freeze on demand, muted by shock. i quickly realize this white-
skinned man is speaking to me and the brown guy seated beside me.
you people... when the man saunters away, anger coils my chest.

the brown guy takes out his phone and carries on as if nothing has
happened.

you people: i am a black girl existing, breathing in canada:

born in toronto, on the east coast, lived here my whole life.

naturally, i assumed i was supposed to belong here.

why?: because my birth certificate identifies me as canadian:
i was *born* here...

> Q: does being born somewhere make it *home*?
> A: a cumulus cloud floating around in my head.

my parents settled in canada, but had previously lived in michigan.
my jamaican-born mom was eight months pregnant upon first arrival
to toronto, canada, in the late 1980s.
to this day my mom sometimes reminds me how close i was to being
born in america.
most times i'm glad i was born in canada instead.

being a canadian with dual identities is a not-so-thrilling brainteaser,
an enigma of sorts:

i'm relegated to a place on the outside looking in
the space between somewhere and nowhere

a blank page: an unchecked box
two misplaced puzzle pieces fitted side by side: made to belong.

12. integration:

once a kenyan girl i met in B.C. called me a "fake african"
because i clumsily peeled an orange with my hands:
as if i had never done that before, as if i had never *had* to
that wasn't the only reason: in her eyes…i was a naive do-gooder, westerner
sitting pretty, and evidently disconnected from my african heritage.

"i'm not a fake african," i repeat myself for the third time in my
spiralling, lonely defence.

as i blabber on, i pray for a mere iota of charm that is said to come with
the number three to fall from the sky, and commandeer my closing
argument.
i get nothing as a substitute instead.

what disqualifies me from africanness:

pick one:
  · i cannot speak the dialect of my father's people.
  · i don't know how to make *fufu* and i dislike the taste of *banku*
  · i don't remember what day ghana's independence falls on
  · I am "canadian-born": a loose term used to identify the children
    born to first-generation ghanaians who have somehow
    acclimated to their western surroundings.
    hashtag: canadianborn—note: not really a compliment.

13. resettlement: i visit the second time because i had become tired
of *not knowing*, of skirting questions about my background.

i longed to identify with the people of my father's homeland and to
know their stories,
to immerse myself in the brilliant complexities of the west african world.

i AM:

a.   the granddaughter of a chief from the akan tribe
b.   my last name quite literally means: "our helper" or "cheerful giver"
c.   i belong to ancestors scattered all over the african diaspora.
d.   named *abena*, because i was born on a tuesday;
      sakyiwaa, in honour of my paternal grandma

  e. i don't need permission to breathe, to *be*
  f. i will not, *cannot* justify my presence in the motherland,
      because she already knows my name.

VESNA JAKSIC LOWE

Sea Creatures

After watching me peel and eat raw barnacles off a rock, my daughter insisted on doing the same. With her right hand, she held onto the ladder that connects the rocky coastline to the Adriatic Sea. With her left hand, she searched for a stone she could use to remove the barnacle, like she saw me doing a minute earlier.

"Is this one okay, Mama?" she said, waving a stone twice the size of her fist.

"Oh, hon, that's too big," I said, motioning for her to drop it into the sea.

Her next pick was a pebble so comically small that I smiled and passed her my stone. She held it tightly and pounded away at the brownish, quarter-sized barnacle glued on the rock in front of her. But the oval creature maintained its stubborn grip on its host, and only muddied the sea around it.

There are some one thousand types of barnacles, and they usually live within shallow waters, where they cling to rocks for life. In Croatian, we call them lupari or lumpari, and they're a common sight for those of us who grew up on the Adriatic coast. More formally, some call them priljepci, where lijepit means "to glue"—a reference to the sticky substance that makes them bond to their habitat. Their slightly cone-shaped shells are greyish or brownish, like the rock formations they adhere to.

They're an odd-looking thing, but their sheer numbers convey a sense of belonging. A single rock can house a dozen or more of them; it's clear they've settled here. They are tethered to their home, and a child's whacks are not enough to sever that bond.

Growing up in Croatia, my dad often walked into the sea below our house with a mesh bag and filled it with lupari. He'd later toss them in a pan with olive oil, garlic, onions, and chopped tomatoes to make sauce for pasta or risotto. Other times, he'd cut up the edible meat with that of other shellfish, then mix it with lemon, olive oil, capers, and scallions to prepare a fresh seafood salad. As kids, my two sisters and I snacked on raw lupari between our swims—I have no doubt we were the subject of some amused British and German tourists taking photos.

Now, watching my daughter wrestle with one of these creatures, I recognized a first-grader's frustration creeping across her tan face. I grabbed the stone from her hand and moved toward another barnacle. Instead of hitting it at the pointy tip of its shell, I approached it from the side and struck it, forcing its sticky hold to relax.

Once I secured it in my hand, I scooped out the circle-shaped meaty part with my index finger, rinsed it out in the sea, and tossed the shell aside. The edge of the meat is dark grey, then gets lighter and sometimes more yellowish toward the centre. It is much smaller, harder, and not nearly as delicious as an oyster, but has that familiar seafood taste I enjoy. I passed it to my daughter, who ate it in one bite.

"Mmmmmm, yummy," she said. "Can I have another?"

We were on Lokrum, a small island outside of Dubrovnik's Old Town, a medieval walled city known as the Pearl of the Adriatic and, more recently, a *Game of Thrones* set. To me, Dubrovnik is a place I call home even though I have not lived there in three decades.

My family left when I was thirteen and Yugoslavia—of which Croatia was a part—was turning into a war zone. We immigrated to Canada, and after finishing high school there, I moved to the United States for college. But I still return to my Croatian hometown every summer vacation.

It's always hot and sunny there in August, and I love swimming in the bay where I grew up. A pedestrian path sprinkled with pine needles hugs the cove, where shades of green and turquoise waters gradually darken into deeper blues. Mediterranean homes with red terracotta roofs line the footpath, with bougainvillea and pine trees creating shade on the stone terraces. With towels slung across their shoulders, kids walk to their favourite swim spots without grown-ups in sight. Stray cats sprawl on the trail, oblivious to the postcard views of the sea around them.

When I'm not eating raw barnacles, I snorkel and search for colourful sea urchin shells. On a good day, I'll find a perfectly intact green or reddish one, then take a deep breath before diving to the bottom to remove the delicate casing with my hand, careful not to let the black needles prick me. Occasionally, I'll stumble upon haliotis, the ear-shaped sparkling shells I like to collect.

There is no sand here—Croatia's coastline is unapologetically rocky. I walk right in, but the tourists wobble in their squeaky water shoes, their arms stretched to the side for balance as they shift from one rock to the next. But I know the pattern of the waves here, know which rocks are smooth and which sway under my feet. I know the nook where the crabs hide, know how close I can get near them before they scatter.

The absence of sand means the Adriatic Sea is so clear, I can see the bottom from even the deepest spot in the bay. It leaves a comforting taste of salt on my tongue and a white trail on my shoulders when I emerge and lounge on a rock to dry off.

This is the only time of the year when my husband and I are not under work deadlines and not schlepping our seven-year-old to soccer, basketball, or whatever her latest obsession is. But there are other pressures and deadlines I feel on our trip, my annual pilgrimage to the motherland. Pressure to immerse my only child in my mother tongue. And deadlines because our time is compressed, no matter how many vacation days we string together.

My husband is American, and my parents and most of my relatives from the former Yugoslavia live outside the United States, so I am hyperaware that the responsibility to connect my daughter with my heritage falls to me, leaving me with both a sense of guilt and nostalgia. I've lived in North America for most of my life and have forgotten many Croatian words and been removed from my culture, and I don't want the same for my daughter. Thanks to her, I've made more of an effort to embrace my background.

So, when I take her to the Euromarket store in New York's Astoria neighborhood, I buy her the same Bajadera and Tortica chocolates I've enjoyed since my childhood. And when we visit my parents in Toronto, I love how she savours my dad's black risotto for dinner. But I'm frustrated when I speak to her in Croatian and she responds almost exclusively in English. When I suggest Croatian lessons, she shakes her head *No!* As an immigrant raising a child in America, my efforts sometimes seem fruitless.

I want her to spend time with my aunt and uncle, to eat freshly caught fish, to bounce in the sea waves, away from the constraints of an American pool staffed by whistling lifeguards. I want her to play with turtles in my childhood home's garden and feed them the same orange flowers I did when I was her age. I want her to absorb the hard consonants of my native language, let them roll off her American tongue. I want my child to see my childhood and cherish it as I do. There are moments when she does. At a restaurant in Dubrovnik last summer, she gulped down octopus salad with such speed that my husband and I had to compete for a bite. After that appetizer, I wiped black stains off her cheeks as she devoured squid ink risotto. But two weeks later, we were at a restaurant in Connecticut, and all she wanted was mac and cheese. We won't be over jet lag yet, but she'll have already transitioned to her American self.

For her, Connecticut is home, and Croatia is a fun place she visits in the summer. There is no nostalgia and longing for the past, no push-and-pull of immigration, no sadness and regret about living an ocean away from your homeland. Her identity is not fractured by a war, her personality not splintered by continents. She has no concept of a present shaped by a past, and her biggest *What if* revolves around what happens if she tries an ice-cream flavour she doesn't like.

I don't think America will ever earn the label of "home" for me, no matter how many years and decades it owns my address. America sends me to a different airport line from my American husband and daughter. America fingerprints me every time I enter its borders, checks my documents with the Department of Homeland Security because it equates immigrants with danger. America called me a "foreign alien" before promoting me to "permanent resident." It is my host country, but our relationship is a rocky one. I permanently reside here, but my sense of belonging is perpetually murky.

What if the war never happened? What if I returned and raised my daughter there? What if we had never left?

In America, I'm the one with the accent, the name that gets mangled. The one who answers your simple questions about my background with geography and history lessons, and whose name you'll forget within minutes of us meeting. The one who's from the place you don't know much about, except for what you read in a travel magazine, but you have things you want to tell me about it anyway. I am unmoored and divided, like the nation that birthed me.

I've spent my whole adult life in the United States, so my English is better than my Croatian. I know my way around, know the lingo, know how to manoeuvre the culture and social norms. But nothing here feels as familiar or clear as a swim in the Adriatic. Even if I'm having fun with friends at a barbecue, a piece of me is missing, or something feels out of place. In America, I'm the unsteady tourist struggling to find my way. Decades away from my motherland have loosened my grip, but I'm the strange creature still clinging to my home.

Acknowledgements

First and foremost, we would like to thank Hazel Millar and Jay MillAr for their support in our vision and for giving this book a home with Book*hug Press. We are grateful for the faith and trust you placed in us. Our gratitude extends to Shannon Whibbs for copy editing, to Ingrid Paulson for the type and design, and to everyone else involved in the production of this book. Taking an idea from concept to bookstore is a huge undertaking requiring the passion of so many others along the printing and distribution chain. We thank you all.

We're deeply grateful to the writers and editors who enthusiastically shared their support and expertise along the way. Thank you to Bonnie Nish, who fanned the flames of what was just an idea of a book, and who provided space for conversations around these themes at Pandora's Collective and Word Vancouver events. You are a gem of a friend and the champion everyone needs in their life. Thank you to Ayelet Tsabari, who believed in this anthology from the beginning and generously shared her time and knowledge to help us get it off the ground. And thank you to Samantha McCabe and Pandemic University for helping gather submissions, and Shereen Zinck and the Edmonton Community Foundation for helping us expand our collection.

Many thanks to our friends and families. Your celebratory notes at every step of this journey warmed our hearts.

This book wouldn't be *this* book that we are so proud of without the contributors and their willingness to explore these ideas with such vulnerability and dedication. Writers, thank you for your beautiful stories.

Biographies

TASLIM JAFFER is a writer, editor, and writing instructor with an MFA in creative nonfiction from the University of King's College. Her bylines include *Maclean's*, *Asparagus*, *WestCoast Families*, CBC British Columbia, *Peace Arch News*, *Unearth Women*, and more. She is the winner of the 2022 Creative Nonfiction Contest from the Creative Nonfiction Collective and *Humber Literary Review*, and recipient of a 2021 Silver Canadian Online Publishing Award. Jaffer has been a keynote speaker on diversity and interfaith topics on a variety of stages and teaches creative nonfiction and expressive writing in community and rehabilitative settings. She is working on a debut collection of literary essays and lives in Surrey, British Columbia, with her husband and three children.

OMAR MOUALLEM is an author, filmmaker, and educator. His journalism has appeared in *The Guardian*, *WIRED*, and the *Wall Street Journal*. His book *How Muslims Shaped the Americas* won the 2022 Wilfred Eggleston Award for Nonfiction and was named one of the *Globe and Mail*'s one hundred best books of 2021. His documentary *The Lebanese Burger Mafia*, which documents the unlikely link between fast food and

Lebanese immigrants, won the 2023 Audience Choice for Best Doc at NorthwestFest. He also teaches creative nonfiction at the University of King's College and is the "fake dean" of Pandemic University School of Writing, a virtual school he founded in support of writers affected by the COVID-19 pandemic. He lives in Edmonton.

CONTRIBUTORS

NADINE ARAKSI is an Armenian-Canadian writer whose work explores womanhood, identity, and the transformative power of storytelling. Her writing has appeared in Canadian publications such as *Chatelaine*, *Maclean's*, *Today's Parent*, and *Canadian Geographic*. Nadine finds inspiration in Toronto's diverse and vibrant neighbourhoods, where she lives with her two teenagers and her faithful feline, Cookie.

OFELIA BROOKS is a Black, Latiné, first-generation writer and lawyer. Her writing has appeared in *Electric Literature*, *Catapult*, *Cutleaf*, *Insider*, and the anthology *Mamas, Martyrs, and Jezebels* (Black Lawrence Press). Her essay "Mother Tongue" was nominated for the Pushcart Prize. She lives in Chicago.

ESMERALDA CABRAL's travel memoir *How to Clean a Fish and Other Adventures in Portugal* was published in Spring 2023 and shortlisted for the Sunshine Coast Writers and Editors Society Nonfiction Prize for B.C. authors. Her writing has been published in the *Globe and Mail*, *Understorey Magazine*, *Gávea-Brown*, *The Common*, *Canadian Traveller*, *Curiosity Magazine*, and nine anthologies. She is a graduate of the

Writer's Studio at Simon Fraser University and holds an MFA in creative nonfiction from the University of King's College in Halifax. Esmeralda was born in the Azores, Portugal, grew up in Alberta, and now lives in Vancouver.

JUNE CHUA was born on the island of Borneo and grew up in Alberta. She worked for two decades at the CBC as a reporter, producer, and news writer/editor, where she also crafted monthly columns. She has directed independent award-winning documentaries and written articles for national newspapers and magazines. Her essays have appeared in *Strangers in the Mirror* and the Best of rabble.ca. She currently resides in Berlin, Germany.

SEEMA DHAWAN is a Calgary-based journalist who has contributed to *USA TODAY, Condé Nast Traveler*, and *Huffington Post*, where she was an editor. Dhawan holds an MFA in creative nonfiction and is working on a collection of essays about her grandparents' pickle empire.

KRISTA EIDE's fiction and creative nonfiction have appeared in publications across Canada. She lives on unceded Musqueam, Squamish, and Tsleil-Waututh territories (Vancouver, British Columbia), where she is the managing editor of *EVENT* magazine and works in film and television.

OMAR EL AKKAD is an author and journalist. His first novel, *American War*, was translated into thirteen languages and is an international bestseller. It was selected by the BBC as one of one hundred novels that shaped our world. His second novel, *What Strange Paradise*, won the Scotiabank Giller Prize, the Oregon Book Award, and the Pacific Northwest Book Award. He lives in the woods just south of Portland, Oregon.

EUFEMIA FANTETTI is the author of *My Father, Fortune-tellers & Me: A Memoir*, and *A Recipe for Disaster & Other Unlikely Tales of Love*, winner of the Bressani Prize for Short Fiction and runner-up for the Danuta Gleed Literary Award. The anthology she co-edited with Ayelet Tsabari and Leonarda Carranza, *Tongues: On Longing and Belonging through Language* (Book*hug Press), won Gold from the 2022 IPPY Awards and Silver from the 2021 Foreword INDIES Book Awards. Her nonfiction has been published in various anthologies, including *Conspicuous Accents, Flash Nonfiction Funny, Love Me True*, and *Body & Soul*. She lives in Toronto, where she teaches creative writing at Humber College and is co-editor of the *Humber Literary Review*.

AYESHA HABIB is a writer and photographer based in Vancouver, British Columbia. She has been a journalist and editor for publications such as the *Globe and Mail, Chatelaine, Toronto Life, Capital Daily*, and *Maisonneuve*. In 2021, Habib self-published a photography zine called *Papercut* and directed the experimental short film *i hope you find the person you want to drown in*. She lives with her exceptionally loud cat.

CHRISTINA HOAG is the author of novels *Girl on the Brink*, named *Suspense Magazine*'s Best of YA; and *Skin of Tattoos*, a Silver Falchion Award finalist; *Law of the Jungle*; and *The Blood Room*, an Audible bestseller. She also co-authored *Peace in the Hood: Working with Gang Members to End the Violence*. Her short stories and essays have been published in numerous literary reviews, including *Toasted Cheese, Lunch Ticket, Other Side of Hope*, and *Shooter*, and have won several awards. Hoag is a former journalist for the *Miami Herald* and foreign correspondent in Latin America, where she reported for *TIME, Business Week, Sunday Times* (London), and the *New York Times*, among other media. She lives in Los Angeles.

MARIAM IBRAHIM is a second-generation Palestinian-Canadian with roots in the Occupied West Bank and Hamilton, Ontario, the traditional territory of the Erie, Neutral, Huron-Wendat, Haudenosaunee, and Mississaugas. She is a writer, editor, and former award-winning newspaper reporter who has appeared as a radio and television commentator. She is the co-founder of two Palestinian human rights organizations and has delivered presentations on the Palestinian issue to diverse audiences. Ibrahim currently lives in Seoul, South Korea, with her husband and aging cat.

VESNA JAKSIC LOWE is a writer and communications consultant for non-profit organizations that promote human rights and social justice. She grew up in the former Yugoslavia and has written about her immigrant experience for the *Connecticut Literary Anthology 2023*, the *New York Times*, the *Washington Post*, the *New York Daily News*, *Catapult*, and *Pigeon Pages*. She runs a monthly newsletter on immigrant literature, *Immigrant Strong*, and has taught on the topic for Rutgers University's Cooper Street Writing Workshops. She participated in Martha's Vineyard Institute of Creative Writing's conference as a first-prize parent-fellow. She lives in Old Greenwich, Connecticut.

KATHRYN GWUN-YEEN LENNON is a writer and editor, born and based in Edmonton/Amiskwacîwâskahikan, with mixed Hong Kong Cantonese and Irish ancestry. Her poetry has been published in *Canthius*, *Brickyard Spoken Word*, *The Polyglot*, *Living Hyphen*, the *Globe and Mail*, *Ricepaper Magazine*, and *The Ethnic Aisle*. Her nonfiction has been published in *Spacing* and *Alternatives Journal*. Her work has been included in several anthologies, including *Reimagining Fire: The Future of Energy*. She is the co-founder and co-editor of *Hungry Zine* and was a member of Edmonton's 2012 Slam Poetry Team.

DIMITRI NASRALLAH is the author of four novels, including *The Bleeds, Niko, Blackbodying,* and the national bestseller *Hotline,* which was nominated for the Scotiabank Giller Prize and shortlisted for CBC's Canada Reads. He was born in Lebanon in 1977 and moved to Canada in 1988. He lives in Montreal, where he serves as fiction editor for Véhicule Press's Esplanade Fiction imprint and teaches creative writing at Concordia University.

LISHAI PEEL is a Hamilton, Ontario-based writer, community-engaged artist, and consultant with over a decade of experience in the arts and culture sector. Her writing has won awards from the Writers' Trust of Canada, *The Malahat Review,* and Vancouver Writers Fest. Her essays and poems have appeared in *Room Magazine, Lilith Magazine, Hey Alma, Middleground, Arc Poetry Magazine, The Malahat Review, Ilanot Review,* and more. Peel has an MFA in creative writing from the University of Guelph and is the inaugural Poet in Place for the City of Hamilton.

OMAR REYES divides his time between writing and social work. His interviews with notable artists and luminaries have appeared in *Georgie Magazine.* He also co-pastors a church called A Beautiful Table, where people can reclaim a more liberating and inclusive faith. Reyes lives with his wife and three sons in Edmonton.

MAHTA RIAZI is a poet, community worker, and educator living in Tkaronto/Toronto. She is the winner of the 2022 *Briarpatch Magazine* Writing in the Margins contest, and her poetry and short fiction have been shortlisted for the Vallum Poetry Award and longlisted for the Nona Macdonald Heaslip Award. She is inspired by and indebted to the poetry of Kristin Chang, Forough Farokhzaad, Sayeh, Hieu Minh

Nguyen, George Abraham, and Joshua Bennett, among others. You can find her work in *Plenitude Magazine, Acta Victoriana, Yolk Literary Journal, Bahr Magazine,* and *Brickplight,* among others. Her chapbook *Parastoo* was published in June 2022 by Cactus Press.

STEVEN SANDOR is an award-winning writer and magazine editor. In 2015, he was named Alberta Magazine Publishers Association Editor of the Year. He is the author of two books on hockey history and eight young adult novels. He has received two commendations from the Canadian Children's Book Centre. A new book on hockey and race will be published in 2025. Sandor lives in Edmonton, where he is the editor-in-chief of *Edify* magazine.

ANGELO SANTOS is a writer, filmmaker, and physiotherapist who has lived in various places around the world, including the Philippines, the Middle East, the United States, and Canada. In 2020, he was selected as a mentee for the Writers' Union of Canada BIPOC Writers Connect conference. Angelo's work has been published in *Ricepaper Magazine, filling Station Magazine,* and *Magdaragat,* an anthology of Filipinx-Canadian writing. He lives in Oakville, Ontario.

ALISON TEDFORD SEAWEED is a Kwakiutl First Nation member and lives in Abbotsford, British Columbia. She has published three business books, including the *Canadian Business Owner's Guide to Reconciliation* and a middle-grade textbook sharing the teachings of Indigenous creative professionals. Her essays have appeared in *Broadview Magazine, Al Jazeera,* CBC, *Today's Parent, Best Health Magazine, Business in Vancouver's* Indigenous edition, and more. She works as a consultant in communications and Indigenous relations and is a graduate student at Simon Fraser University.

MAKDA TESHOME was born and lives in Toronto, Ontario. In 2020, she graduated from the University of Toronto with a BAS(c) in criminology, sociolegal studies, and history. She works in program management and takes pride in coordinating events and programs centred on social justice and urban development. New to the literary world, Teshome has written one other piece on the Ethiopian pentatonic scale, "Tizita," for *Tillism*. She hopes to continue writing fiction and nonfiction pieces centring on the immigrant and first-generation experience.

NHUNG N. TRAN-DAVIES is an author, physician, mother of three, and advocate for social justice in education. She came to Canada as a refugee from the Vietnam War when she was a young child. She loves to write children's stories that convey the humanity in our lives, and the themes of her books include refugees and immigration, poverty, and the power of kindness and education. She is the author of three picture books, *Ten Cents a Pound*, *The Doll*, and *Green Papayas*, as well as the middle-grade/YA novel, *A Grain of Rice*. Her books have been shortlisted for the Alberta Literary Awards, the Red Maple Award, the Blue Spruce Award, and the TD Canadian Children's Literature Award. She currently lives in Calmar, Alberta.

ALEXANDRA C. YEBOAH is a Brampton, Ontario-based writer, creative facilitator, wanderlust, and quiet disruptor. A second-generation Canadian to immigrant parents, Yeboah writes about bicultural identity and how it intersects with everyday experiences, self-acceptance, growth, and playful discovery. Her print project, *Breaking Barriers,* was published by the Mayworks Festival in 2021. She currently sits on the Festival of Literary Diversity's advisory council board.

HANNAH ZALAA-UUL (she/her) is a Mongolian writer of short stories, personal essays, and poetry. With a degree in international development and two years of professional experience in the field, she works in the non-profit sector as a program officer coordinating sustainable water, sanitation, and hygiene projects for communities across West Africa and Southeast Asia. Zalaa-Uul is dedicated to storytelling that bridges connections across generations and nationalities, offering a glimpse into shared human experiences. She lives in Toronto.

Colophon

Manufactured as the first edition of
Back Where I Came From: On Culture, Identity, and Home
in the fall of 2024 by Book*hug Press

Copy-edited by Shannon Whibbs
Proofread by Laurie Siblock
Type + design by Ingrid Paulson

Printed in Canada

bookhugpress.ca